D0916865

Fighting Infectious Diseases

ROSEN
PUBLISHING®

New York

Published in 2007 by The Rosen Publishing Group, Inc.
29 East 21st Street, New York, NY 10010

The articles in this book first appeared in the pages of *Scientific American*, as
follows: "If Smallpox Strikes Portland . . ." by Chris L. Barrett, Stephen G.
Eubank and James P. Smith, March 2005; "Can Chlamydia Be Stopped?" by
David M. Ojcius, Toni Darville and Patrik M. Bavoil, May 2005; "Attacking
Anthrax" by John A. T. Young and R. John Collier, March 2002; "Detecting
Mad Cow Disease" by Stanley B. Prusiner, July 2004; "Hope in a Vial" by Carol
Ezzell, June 2002; "Edible Vaccines" by William H. R. Langridge, September
2000; "Beyond Chicken Soup" by William A. Haseltine, November 2001.

First Edition

Library of Congress Cataloging-in-Publication Data

Fighting infectious diseases.
    p. cm.—(Scientific American cutting-edge science)
Includes index.
ISBN-13: 978-1-4042-0988-6
ISBN-10: 1-4042-0988-3 (library binding)
1. Communicable diseases. 2. Infection. I. Scientific American.
RC112.F49 2007
616.9—dc22

                                                    2006024273

Manufactured in the United States of America

On the cover: This is one part of an illustration from the article "Hope in a
Vial" demonstrating how an immune response would be elicited in a vaccine
strategy for AIDS. Here, a cytotoxic T cell activates immune cells to produce
antibodies or kill infected cells.

Illustration credits: Cover, p. 90 Terese Winslow; pp. 10 (top), 16 Lucy
Reading-Ikkanda; pp. 10 (bottom), 11 Stephen G. Eubank; pp. 30–31 Source:
www.med.sc.edu:85/mayer/chlamyd.htm; pp. 34–35 © Andrew Swift; pp. 52–53
© Bryan Christie Design; pp. 63, 68–69 Lucy Reading; p. 67 Sources:
International Organization for Epizootic Diseases/World Health Organization/
University of California, San Francisco; pp. 86–87 Laurie Grace/Sources:
UNAIDS (statistics) and Vadim Zalunin Los Alamos National Laboratory
(clade boundaries); pp. 104, 110–111, 114 Jared Schneidman Design.

Contents

I. "If Smallpox Strikes Portland . . ."

by Chris L. Barrett, Stephen G. Eubank
and James P. Smith

"Episims" unleashes virtual plagues in real cities to see how social networks spread disease. That knowledge might help stop epidemics

Suppose terrorists were to release plague in Chicago, and health officials, faced with limited resources and personnel, had to quickly choose the most effective response. Would mass administration of antibiotics be the best way to halt an outbreak? Or mass quarantines? What if a chance to nip a global influenza pandemic in the bud meant sending national stockpiles of antiviral drugs to Asia where a deadly new flu strain was said to be emerging? If the strategy succeeded, a worldwide crisis would be averted; if it failed, the donor countries would be left with less protection.

Public health officials have to make choices that could mean life or death for thousands, even millions, of people, as well as massive economic and social disruption. And history offers them only a rough guide. Methods that eradicated smallpox in African villages in the 1970s, for example, might not be the most effective tactics against smallpox released in a U.S. city in the 21st century. To identify the best responses under a variety of conditions in advance of disasters, health officials need a laboratory where "what if" scenarios can be tested as realistically as possible. That is why our group at Los Alamos National Laboratory (LANL) set out to build EpiSims, the largest individual-based epidemiology simulation model ever created.

Modeling the interactions of each individual in a population allows us to go beyond estimating the number of people likely to be infected; it lets us simulate the paths a disease would take through the population and thus where the outbreak could be intercepted most effectively. The networks that support everyday life and provide employment, transportation infrastructure, necessities and luxuries are the same ones that infectious diseases exploit to spread among human hosts. By modeling this social network in fine detail, we can understand its structure and how to alter it to disrupt the spread of disease while inflicting the least damage to the social fabric.

Virtual Epidemiology

LONG BEFORE the germ theory of disease, London physician John Snow argued that cholera, which had killed tens of thousands of people in England during the preceding 20 years, spread via the water supply. In the summer of 1854 he tested that theory during an outbreak in the Soho district. On a map, he marked the location of the homes of each of the 500 victims who had died in the preceding 10 days and noted where each victim had gotten water. He discovered that every one of them drank water from the Broad

Street pump, so Snow convinced officials to remove the pump handle. His action limited the death toll to 616.

Tracing the activities and contacts of individual disease victims, as Snow did, remains an important tool for modern epidemiologists. And it is nothing new for health authorities to rely on models when developing policies to protect the public. Yet most mathematical models for understanding and predicting the course of disease outbreaks describe only the interactions of large numbers of people in aggregate. One reason is that modelers have often lacked detailed knowledge of how specific contagious diseases spread. Another is that they have not had realistic models of the social interactions in which people have contact with one another. And a third is that they have not had the computational and methodological means to build models of diseases interacting with dynamic human populations.

As a result, epidemiology models typically rely on estimates of a particular disease's "reproductive

Overview/Simulating Society

- Epidemiological simulations provide virtual laboratories where health officials can test the effectiveness of different responses in advance of disease outbreaks.
- Modeling the movements of every individual in a large population produces a dynamic picture of the social network—the same network of contacts used by infectious diseases to spread among human hosts.
- Knowing the paths a disease could take through society enables officials to alter the social network through measures such as school closings and quarantines or by targeting individuals for medical treatment.

number"—the number of people likely to be infected by one contagious person or contaminated location. Often this reproductive number is a best guess based on historical situations, even though the culture, physical conditions and health status of people in those events may differ greatly from the present situation.

In real epidemics, these details matter. The rate at which susceptible people become infected depends on their individual state of health, the duration and nature of their interactions with contagious people, and specific properties of the disease pathogen itself. Truer models of outbreaks must capture the probability of disease transmission from one person to another, which means simulating not only the properties of the disease and the health of each individual but also detailed interactions between every pair of individuals in the group.

Attempts to introduce such epidemiological models have, until recently, considered only very small groups of 100 to 1,000 people. Their size has been limited because they are based on actual populations, such as the residents, visitors and staff of a nursing home, so they require detailed data about individuals and their contacts over days or weeks. Computing such a large number of interactions also presents substantial technical difficulties.

Our group was able to construct this kind of individual-based epidemic model on a scale of millions of people by using high-performance supercomputing clusters and by building on an existing model called

TRANSIMS developed over more than a decade at Los Alamos for urban planning [see "Unjamming Traffic with Computers," by Kenneth R. Howard; SCIENTIFIC AMERICAN, October 1997]. The TRANSIMS project started as a means of better understanding the potential effects of creating or rerouting roads and other transportation infrastructure. By giving us a way to simulate the movements of a large population through a realistic urban environment, TRANSIMS provided the foundation we needed to model the interactions of millions of individuals for EpiSims.

Although EpiSims can now be adapted to different cities, the original TRANSIMS model was based on Portland, Ore. The TRANSIMS virtual version of Portland incorporates detailed digital maps of the city, including representations of its rail lines, roads, signs, traffic signals and other transportation infrastructure, and produces information about traffic patterns and travel times. Publicly available data were used to generate 180,000 specific locations, a synthetic population of 1.6 million residents, and realistic daily activities for those people.

Integrating all this information into a computer model provides the best estimate of physical contact patterns for large human populations ever created. With EpiSims, we can release a virtual pathogen into these populations, watch it spread and test the effects of different interventions. But even without simulating a disease outbreak, the model provides intriguing insights into human social networks, with potentially important implications for epidemic response.

Social Networks

TO UNDERSTAND what a social network really is and how it can be used for epidemiology, imagine the daily activities and contacts of a single hypothetical adult, Ann. She has short brushes with family members during breakfast and then with other commuters or carpoolers on her way to work. Depending on her job, she might meet dozens of people at work, with each encounter having a different duration, proximity and purpose. During lunch or a shopping trip after work, Ann might have additional short contacts with strangers in public places before returning home.

We can visually represent Ann's contacts as a network with Ann in the center and a line connecting Ann to each of them [see *illustration on pages 10–11*]. All Ann's contacts engage in various activities and meet other people as well. We can represent these "contacts of contacts" by drawing lines from each— for example, Ann's colleague named Bob—to all his contacts. Unless they are also contacts of Ann, Bob's contacts are two "hops" away from Ann. The number of hops on the shortest path between people is some-times called the graph distance or degree of separation between those people.

The popular idea that everyone on the earth is connected to everyone else by at most six degrees of

Building Social Networks

TYPICAL HOUSEHOLD'S CONTACTS

Constructing a social network for a household of two adults and two children starts by identifying their contacts with other people throughout a typical day.

This diagram shows where the household members go and what they do all day but reveals little about how their individual contacts might be interconnected or connected to others.

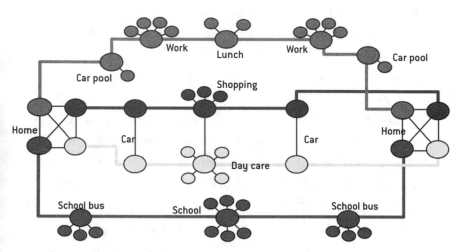

LOCAL SOCIAL NETWORK

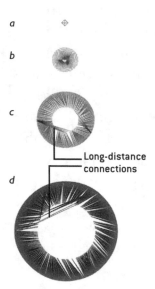

A social network emerges by drawing lines to represent connections within the household (a) and from the household members to their direct contacts (b). Connecting those individuals to their own circle of contacts (c) and those to the next generation of contacts (d) enlarges the network. Long-distance connections show contacts who also know each other. Yet no one in this network has more than 15 direct contacts, meaning none is a highly connected "hub" of society. One insight from this work is that so many alternative paths can connect any pair of people, isolating only hub individuals would do little to restrict the spread of infectious disease through this population.

EXPANDER GRAPH
The shape of this small network expands with each generation of contacts. A disease moving through such a population therefore infects rising numbers of people in each generation of transmission.

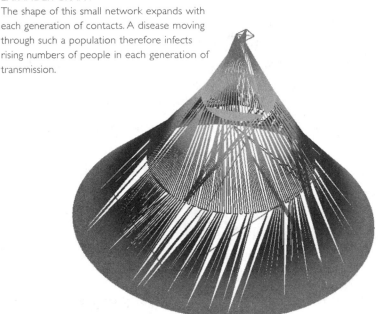

separation means that if we continued building our social network until it included everyone on the planet, no two people would be more than six hops from one another. The idea is not strictly true, but it makes for a good story and has even led to the well-known game involving the social network of actors who have appeared in films with Kevin Bacon. In academic circles, another such social network traces mathematicians' co-authorship connections, with one's "Erdös number" defined by graph distance from the late, brilliant and prolific Paul Erdös.

Other types of networks, including the Internet, the links among scientific article citations and even

Fighting Infectious Diseases

the interactions among proteins within living cells, have been found to display this same tendency toward having "hubs": certain locations, people or even molecules with an unusually high number of connections to the rest of the network. The shortest path between any two nodes in the network is typically through one of these hubs, much as in a commercial airline's route system. Technically, such networks are called "scale-free" when the number of hubs with exactly k connections, N(k), is proportional to a power of k [see "Scale-Free Networks," by Albert-László Barabási and Eric Bonabeau; SCIENTIFIC AMERICAN, May 2003].

Because a scale-free network can be severely damaged if one or more of its hubs are disabled, some researchers have extrapolated this observation to disease transmission. If infected "hub" individuals, such as the most gregarious people in a population, could somehow be identified and treated or removed from the network, the reasoning goes, then an epidemic could be halted without having to isolate or treat everyone in the population. But our analyses of the social networks used by EpiSims suggest that society is not so easily disabled as physical infrastructure.

The network of physical locations in our virtual Portland, defined by people traveling between them, does indeed exhibit the typical scale-free structure, with certain locations acting as important hubs. As a result, these locations, such as schools and shopping malls, would be good spots for disease surveillance or for placing sensors to detect the presence of biological agents.

The urban social networks in the city also have human hubs with higher than average contacts, many because they work in the physical hub locations, such as teachers or sales clerks. Yet we have also found an unexpectedly high number of "short paths" in the social networks that do not go through hubs, so a policy of targeting only hub individuals would probably do little to slow the spread of a disease through the city.

In fact, another unexpected property we have found in realistic social networks is that everyone but the most devoted recluse is effectively a small hub. That is to say, when we look at the contacts of any small group, such as four students, we find that they are always connected by one hop to a much larger group. Depicting this social network structure results in what is known as an expander graph [*see illustration on pages 10–11*], which has a cone shape that widens with each hop. Its most important implication for epidemiology is that diseases can disseminate exponentially fast because the number of people exposed in each new generation of transmission is always larger than the number in the current generation.

Theoretically, this should mean that whatever health officials do to intervene in a disease outbreak, speed will be one of the most important factors determining their success. Simulating disease outbreaks with EpiSims allows us to see whether that theory holds true.

Smallpox Attack

AFTER WE BEGAN developing EpiSims in 2000, smallpox was among the first diseases we chose to model because government officials charged with bioterrorism planning and response were faced with several questions and sometimes conflicting recommendations. In the event that smallpox was released into a U.S. population, would mass vaccination be necessary to prevent an epidemic? Or would targeting only exposed individuals and their contacts for vaccination be enough? How effective is mass quarantine? How feasible are any of these options with the existing numbers of health workers, police and other responders?

To answer such questions, we constructed a model of smallpox that we could release into our synthetic population. Smallpox transmission was particularly difficult to model because the virus has not infected humans since its eradication in the 1970s. Most experts agree, though, that the virus normally requires significant physical contact with an infectious person or contaminated object. The disease has an average incubation period of approximately 10 days before flulike symptoms begin appearing, followed by skin rash. Victims are contagious once symptoms have appeared and possibly for a short time before they develop fever. Untreated, some 30 percent of those infected would die, but the rest would recover and be immune to reinfection.

Vaccination before exposure or within four days of infection can stop smallpox from developing. We assumed in all our simulations that health workers and people charged with tracking down the contacts of infected people had already been vaccinated and thus were immune. Unlike many epidemiological models, our realistic simulation also ensures that the chronology of contacts will be considered. If Ann contracted the disease, she could not infect her co-worker Bob a week earlier. Or, if Ann does infect Bob after she herself becomes infected and if Bob in turn infects his family member Cathy, the infection cannot pass from Ann to Cathy in less than twice the minimum incubation period between disease exposure and becoming contagious.

With our disease model established and everyone in our synthetic population assigned an immune status, we simulated the release of smallpox in several hub locations around the city, including a university campus. Initially, 1,200 people were unwittingly infected, and within hours they had moved throughout the city, going about their normal activities.

We then simulated several types of official responses, including mass vaccination of the city's population or contact tracing of exposed individuals and their contacts who could then be targeted for vaccination and quarantine. Finally, we simulated no response at all for the purpose of comparison.

In each of these circumstances, we also simulated delays of four, seven and 10 days in implementing the response after the first victims became known. In addition, we allowed infected individuals to isolate themselves by withdrawing to their homes.

Simulated Smallpox Attacks

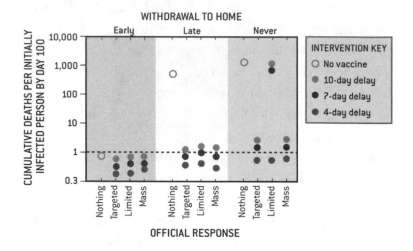

RESPONSE EFFECTIVENESS
Simulations allowed people to withdraw to their homes because they felt ill or were
following officials' instructions. Withdrawal could be "early," before anyone became
contagious, or "never," meaning people continued moving about unless they died.
"Late" withdrawal, 24 hours after becoming contagious, was less effective than early
withdrawal, which prevented an epidemic without other intervention. Official responses
included doing nothing, or targeted vaccination and quarantine with unlimited personnel,
or targeted vaccination limited by only half the necessary personnel being available, or
mass vaccination of the entire population. The interventions began four, seven or 10
days after the first victims became symptomatic.

Each simulation ran for a virtual 100 days, and the
precise casualty figures resulting from each scenario
were less important than the relative effect different
responses had on the death tolls. The results upheld
our theoretical prediction based on the expander-graph
structure of the social network: time was by far the

most important factor in limiting deaths. The speed with which people withdrew to their homes or were isolated by health officials was the strongest determinant of the outbreak's extent. The second most influential factor was the length of the delay in officials' response. The actual response strategy chosen made little difference compared with the time element.

In the case of a smallpox outbreak, these simulations indicate that mass vaccination of the population, which carries its own risks, would be unnecessary. Targeted vaccination would be just as effective so long as it was combined with rapid detection of the outbreak and rapid response. Our results also support the importance of measures such as quarantine and making sure that health officials give enforcement adequate priority during highly infectious disease outbreaks.

Of course, appropriate public health responses will always depend on the disease, the types of interventions available and the setting. For example, we have simulated the intentional release of an inhalable form of plague in the city of Chicago to evaluate the costs and effects of different responses. In those simulations we found that contact tracing, school closures and city closures each incurred economic losses of billions of dollars but did not afford many health benefits over voluntary mass use of rapidly available antibiotics at a much lower economic cost.

Most recently, as part of a research network organized by the National Institute of General Medical Sciences called the Models of Infectious Disease Agent

Study (MIDAS), we have been adapting EpiSims to model a naturally occurring disease that may threaten the entire planet: pandemic influenza.

Flu and the Future

OVER THE PAST YEAR, a highly virulent strain of influenza has raged through bird populations in Asia and has infected more than 40 human beings in Japan, Thailand and Vietnam, killing more than 30 of those people. The World Health Organization has warned that it is only a matter of time before this lethal flu strain, designated H5N1, more easily infects people and spreads between them. That development could spark a global flu pandemic with a death toll reaching tens of millions [see SA Perspectives, SCIENTIFIC AMERICAN, January].

MIDAS collaborators will be studying the possibility that an H5N1 virus capable of spreading in humans might be contained or even eradicated by rapid intervention while it is still confined to a small population. To simulate the appropriate conditions in which the strain would likely emerge among humans, we are constructing a model representing a hypothetical Southeast Asian community of some 500,000 people living on farms and in neighboring small towns. Our model of the influenza virus itself will be based both on historical data about pandemic flu strains and information about the H5N1 virus, whose biology is currently a subject of intense investigation.

We know, for example, that H5N1 is sensitive to antiviral drugs that inhibit one of its important enzymes, called neuraminidase. In our simulations, we will be able to use neuraminidase inhibitors as both treatment and prophylaxis. (A vaccine against H5N1 has been developed and recently began clinical trials but because the vaccine is not yet proven or available, we will focus our simulations on seeing whether the antiviral drugs together with traditional public health measures might stop an epidemic.)

Preliminary results announced in late February are reported at www.sciam.com. In April, we will complete similar flu pandemic simulations in the EpiSims Portland model.

Our hope is that the ability to realistically model populations and disease outbreaks can help health officials make difficult decisions based on the best possible answers to "what if" questions.

The creation of models such as TRANSIMS that simulate human movements through urban environments was the computational breakthrough that made EpiSims possible, and epidemiology is only one potential application for this kind of individual-based modeling. We are also in the process of creating and linking simulations of other sociotechnical systems, including environmental and atmospheric pollution, telecommunications, transportation, commodity markets, water supplies and power grids, to provide virtual laboratories for exploring solutions to a wide variety of real-world problems.

More to Explore

Scalable, Efficient Epidemiological Simulation.
Stephen Eubank in *Proceedings of the 2002
ACM Symposium on Applied Computing*, pages
139–145; 2002.

Six Degrees: The Science of a Connected Age.
Duncan J. Watts. W. W. Norton, 2004.

Containing Pandemic Influenza with Antiviral Agents.
Ira M. Longini, Jr., et al. in *American Journal of
Epidemiology*, Vol. 159, No. 7, pages 623–633;
April 1, 2004.

**Modelling Disease Outbreaks in Realistic Urban
Social Networks.** Stephen Eubank et al. in *Nature*,
Vol. 429, pages 180–184; May 13, 2004.

A sample EpiSims animation and additional data from
the Portland smallpox simulations can be viewed
at **http://episims.lanl.gov**

The Authors

CHRIS L. BARRETT, STEPHEN G. EUBANK and
JAMES P. SMITH worked for five years together at
Los Alamos National Laboratory (LANL) to develop
the EpiSims simulation. Barrett, who oversaw a
predecessor project, TRANSIMS, is a bioinformatics
specialist who now directs the Simulation Science
Laboratory at the Virginia Bioinformatics Institute
(VBI) in Blacksburg. Eubank, a physicist, is deputy
director of the VBI simulation lab and was EpiSims

team leader at Los Alamos. Smith, also a physicist, continues to work with simulations related to TRANSIMS as the project office leader for Discrete Simulation Science in the LANL Computer and Computational Sciences Division.

"Can Chlamydia
2. Be Stopped?"

by David M. Ojcius, Toni Darville and Patrik M. Bavoil

Chlamydia is a rampant sexually transmitted disease, the world's leading cause of preventable blindness and a possible contributor to heart disease. Recent discoveries are suggesting new ways to curtail its spread

Ask the average American about chlamydia, and you will probably evoke an uneasy cringe. Most people think immediately of one of the world's most common sexually transmitted diseases (STDs). But the term actually refers to an entire genus of tiny bacteria that can ignite a variety of serious illnesses.

Ask a poor mother in Africa about chlamydia, and she may tell you that flies transmitting this infection gave her two young children the painful eye condition known as conjunctivitis. This illness—caused by a strain of *Chlamydia trachomatis* (the species that also causes STDs)—can lead to trachoma, a potentially blinding disease. In industrial countries, an airborne species, *C. pneumoniae*, causes colds, bronchitis and about 10 percent of pneumonias acquired outside of hospitals. Researchers have even drawn tentative links between *C. pneumoniae* and atherosclerosis, the artery-narrowing condition that leads to heart attacks and strokes.

Because chlamydiae are bacteria, antibiotics can thwart the infections they produce. Unfortunately, the illnesses often go undetected and untreated, for various reasons. The genital infections rarely produce symptoms early on. And in developing countries where trachoma is a concern, people often lack access to adequate treatment and hygiene. As a result, many of the estimated 600 million people infected with one or more *Chlamydia* strains will go without medical care until the consequences have become irreversible.

It is unrealistic to expect that doctors will ever identify all individuals who have the STD or that improved hygiene will soon wipe out the trachoma-causing bacteria in developing countries. For these reasons, the best hope for curtailing the spread of these ailments is to develop an effective vaccine or other preventive treatments. To discover agents able to block infections before they start, scientists need to know more about how chlamydiae replicate, incite disease and function at a molecular level. But that information has been hard to come by. These bugs are wily. Not only do they have varied strategies for evading the body's immune system, they also are notoriously difficult to study in the laboratory. In the past five years, however, new research—including the complete sequencing of the genomes of several *Chlamydia* strains—has helped scientists begin to address these obstacles. The resulting discoveries are renewing hope for developing new prevention strategies.

Silent Injury

ONE MAJOR IMPEDIMENT to the production of a vaccine is chlamydia's surreptitious way of wreaking havoc on

Cardiovascular Connections

Colds, bronchitis and pneumonia may not be the sole concern for people who have inhaled the airborne species of *Chlamydia*. Recent evidence hints that *C. pneumoniae* infections may also contribute to strokes and heart attacks. Such a link may have an upside, however—doctors might eventually be able to prescribe antibiotics to fight both the infection and the heart disease.

Atherosclerosis—a narrowing of the coronary arteries that leads to most strokes and heart attacks—causes approximately half of all adult deaths in the Western world. But traditional risk factors, such as elevated cholesterol and cigarette smoking, account for only about half of that total. Scientists searching for a reason behind the other 50 percent began to consider infections once it became clear that inflammation—a generalized immune response against any perceived invader—also underlies the growth and destructive ruptures of the fat-laden deposits that constrict coronary arteries [see "Atherosclerosis: The New View," by Peter Libby; SCIENTIFIC AMERICAN, May 2002].

C. pneumoniae became a prime suspect in the condition shortly after it was identified as a separate chlamydial species in 1983. It drew suspicion because of its ubiquity—more than 60 percent of adults worldwide carry antibodies against it (a sign of past or ongoing infection). Support for the hunch emerged in 1988, when physicians in Finland reported a positive correlation between the presence of these antibodies and the risk of developing coronary artery disease; other researchers identified the bacterium in clogged human arteries five years later. Since then, organizations such as the National Institutes of Health and the American Heart Association have invested millions of dollars to study the relation between *C. pneumoniae* and atherosclerosis.

Animal studies conducted within the past five years or so have provided some of the most convincing evidence for a link. One demonstrated, for example, that chlamydial bacteria can move from the lungs of mice to other parts of the body within white blood cells, the agents responsible for inflammation. Other research has shown that *C. pneumoniae* infections accelerate atherosclerosis in both mice and rabbits and that antichlamydial antibiotics can prevent that acceleration.

Experimental results such as these, though tentative, were enough to justify a handful of small clinical trials in humans. Five of these trials showed that one to three months of antibiotic treatment had a statistically significant benefit against the progression of atherosclerosis. But results were mixed as to whether the antibiotics could actually prevent serious cardiac events. The promise for longer-term treatment was also dealt a blow by the negative outcomes of two large trials completed in 2004, each involving 4,000 volunteers who received antibiotics for one to two years.

Establishing whether a clear connection exists between *C. pneumoniae* infection and atherosclerosis in humans may prove difficult simply because so many other factors participate in heart disease. Exactly how troublesome such complications will be, however, remains to be seen.   —*D. M. O., T .D. and P. M. B.*

the body. The microbes that cause tetanus or cholera swamp tissues with toxins that damage or kill vulnerable cells. Chlamydiae, in contrast, do not damage tissues directly. Rather they elicit an enthusiastic immune response that attempts to rein in the infection through inflammation for as long as the bacteria remain in the body—even at low levels. Ironically, this way of fighting the infection actually brings on the long-term damage. Vaccines prevent illness by priming the immune system to react strongly to specific disease-causing agents, but in this case, the inflammatory component of such a response could do more harm than good.

Whether in the genital tract, eyelids or elsewhere, inflammation begins when certain cells of the host immune system secrete factors called cytokines—small signaling proteins that attract additional defensive cells to the site of infection. The attracted cells and the cytokines try to wall off the area to prevent the bacteria's spread. In the skin, this process gives rise to familiar outward manifestations of inflammation: redness, swelling and heat. At the same time, the inflammatory cytokines help to trigger the tissue repair response called fibrosis, which can lead to scarring.

In the genital tract, the early inflammation is not obvious. Of the 3.5 million Americans infected with sexually transmitted chlamydia every year, 85 to 90 percent show no symptoms. Men, whose inflammation occurs in the penis, may experience slight pain during urination; women may feel nothing as the bacteria move up the genital tract into the fallopian tubes. Unaware of the problem, these individuals inadvertently pass the bugs along. Indeed, a woman may not learn of her infection until she tries to become pregnant and realizes she is infertile. In other cases, persistent inflammation and scarring of the fallopian tubes causes chronic pelvic pain or increases the chances of ectopic, or tubal, pregnancy—the leading cause of first-trimester pregnancy-related deaths in the U.S.

Inflammation of the eyelids is more immediately obvious. Such infections afflict an estimated 150 million people living in developing countries with hot climates; there treatments may be scarce, and flies and gnats can readily transmit the bacteria between people's infrequently washed hands and faces. (Trachoma does not occur in the U.S. or western Europe because of better public health systems.) When infections scar the inside of the upper eyelid repeatedly over many years, the eyelid may begin to turn under, pointing the eyelashes inward where they can scratch the cornea. Unchecked, the corneal damage can cause blindness decades after the initial infection.

Given that inflammation accounts for most of chlamydia's ill effects, those who are striving to develop a vaccine must find a way to control the bacteria without inducing a strong inflammatory reaction. Ideally, any intervention would fine-tune the inflammatory response—evoking it just enough to help the body's other immune defenses eliminate the bacteria.

Much research on infections caused by chlamydia and other pathogens is focusing on factors that either initiate secretion of the inflammatory cytokines or dampen the inflammatory response once the infection has been cleared. Over the past few years, investigators have discovered small molecules that normally stimulate or inhibit these responses in the body. The next step will be to develop compounds that are able to regulate the activities of these molecules. These agents might be delivered to shut down inflammation artificially after an antibiotic has been administered to control the bacteria.

Hanging Around

BEYOND INDUCING INFLAMMATION, chlamydiae have other properties that impede development of an effective vaccine. For instance, once you get mumps or measles—or the vaccines against them—you are immune for life. Not so with chlamydia. The body has a hard time eliminating the bacteria completely, and natural immunity after a bout with the microbes lasts only about six months. Hence, an infection that has apparently disappeared may flare up again months or years later, and little protection remains against new outbreaks. If the body's natural response to infection cannot confer long-term protection, it seems likely that a vaccine that merely mimicked this response would fail as well. To be successful, a vaccine would have to elicit defenses that were more powerful than those occurring naturally without triggering excessive inflammation.

One way that vaccines or natural immune responses to an initial infection protect against future colonization by certain microorganisms is by inducing the body to produce so-called memory B lymphocytes targeted to those specific invaders. These immune cells patrol the body throughout its lifetime, ready to secrete antibody molecules that can in turn latch onto any new bugs and mark them for destruction before they invade healthy cells. The antibody system works well against a number of disease-causing agents or pathogens— especially against the many bacteria that live outside a host's cells. In theory, antibodies could attack the microbes before they entered cells or when newly minted copies traveled from one cell to another. But the B lymphocyte system is not terribly effective at these tasks when it comes to chlamydiae, which live inside the cells, where circulating antibodies cannot reach them.

To prevent chlamydiae from lying dormant in cells and then

- Chlamydia has many modes of attack. Untreated infections have blinded more than six million people worldwide, leave more than 10,000 women in the U.S. sterile every year, and account for 10 percent of pneumonia cases in industrial countries.
- Most people affected by chlamydia are not treated with antibiotics until after the damage is done; either they do not notice their symptoms right away, or they do not have access to adequate hygiene or health care.
- Global sex education campaigns and improved hygiene can certainly help limit the bacterium's spread, but other preventive measures such as vaccines are probably the only way to stamp out the disease entirely.

proliferating anew, a vaccine would probably need to pump up the so-called cellular arm of the immune system in addition to evoking an antibody attack. This arm, critical to eradicating viruses (which also live inside cells), relies on killer and helper T cells as well as on scavenger cells known as macrophages to eliminate invaders. Unfortunately, even this trio of immune cells does an incomplete job of eliminating chlamydiae, too often allowing infected cells to survive and become bacteria-producing factories.

Developing a vaccine able to evoke a better cellular response than the body could mount on its own is a tall order. Most existing vaccines elicit a targeted antibody response, but safely activating cellular immunity against many infectious diseases remains a challenging task. The job is particularly difficult in the case of chlamydiae because these bacteria have special ways of protecting themselves from attack by the cellular branch of the immune system.

Hidden Hijackers

LIKE CERTAIN OTHER bacterial pathogens, chlamydiae induce epithelial cells—in this case, those lining genital tracts, eyelids or lungs—to absorb them within a membrane-bound sac, or vacuole. Healthy cells typically attempt to kill internalized pathogens by having the entry vacuoles fuse with lysosomes, cellular structures containing enzymes that chop up proteins, lipids and DNA. All cells display the chopped-up pieces on

Chlamydia Is Not Just an STD

SPECIES	DISEASE	DISTRIBUTION
C. pneumoniae	Pneumonia; possibly atherosclerosis	Worldwide
C. psittaci	Psittacosis, a flulike infection of the lungs that can cause inflammation of the liver, heart and brain	Worldwide
C. trachomatis (Different strains cause different disorders.)	Trachoma, a painful eye infection that begins as conjunctivitis and leads to scarring of the cornea and possible blindness	Southeast Asia, South America, India, Middle East, Africa; rare in the U.S.
C. trachomatis	Sexually transmitted disease (STD) of the adult genital tract; can cause conjunctivitis and pneumonia in newborns	Worldwide
C. trachomatis	Lymphogranuloma venereum, an STD of the lymph glands in the genital area	Asia, Africa, South America, Central America; rare in the U.S.

proteins called major histocompatibility complex (MHC) molecules at the cell surface. Killer and helper T cells, which travel around the body continuously, will then glom on to MHC molecules that display bits of foreign proteins. If the T cells also receive other indications of trouble, they will deduce that the cells are infected and will orchestrate an attack on them.

MODE OF TRANSMISSION	NUMBERS AFFECTED
Inhalation of the bacterium within aerosols produced when an infected person coughs	Causes about 10 percent of pneumonia cases in developed countries, including up to 300,000 new cases in the U.S. every year
Inhalation of the bacterium in aerosols or dust; a bite from or handling the plumage or tissues of an infected bird	Common in wild and domestic birds; rare but potentially fatal when transmitted to humans; 50 to 100 new human cases in the U.S. every year
Direct contact with bodily secretions of infected people or contact with carrier flies or clothing contaminated with such secretions	More than 500 million people worldwide have trachoma, and seven million to nine million are blind as a result of it; virtually no incidence in areas with adequate hygiene
Sexual contact; newborns acquire the bacterium from their infected mothers while passing through the birth canal	50 million to 90 million new STD infections occur globally every year; in the U.S. alone, 3.5 million new infections and more than 10,000 cases of female infertility
Sexual contact	Global incidence is unknown; 300 to 500 cases in the U.S. every year

But chlamydiae somehow compel their entry vacuoles to avoid lysosomes, enabling the bacteria to proliferate freely while separated physically from the rest of the infected cell. If the lysosomes cannot provide bits of the bacteria for display on the cell surface, patrolling T cells will not recognize that a cell harbors invaders. Understanding how the bacteria grow and avoid lysosomes might suggest new ways to forestall or halt the infection. Recent findings, including the newly sequenced *Chlamydia* genomes, are aiding in that effort.

The sequence of genetic building blocks in an organism's DNA specifies the proteins that cells make; the proteins, in turn, carry out most cellular activities. Thus, the sequence of codes in a gene says a good deal about how an organism functions. Researchers, including Ru-ching Hsia and one of us (Bavoil) of the University of Maryland, discovered a particularly important element of chlamydiae by noting similarities between their genes and those of larger bacteria, such as *Salmonella typhimurium*, infamous for causing food poisoning. Scientists now generally agree that chlamydiae have everything they need to form a versatile, needlelike projection called a type III secretion apparatus. This apparatus, which spans the membrane of the entry vacuole, serves as a conduit between the bacteria and the cytoplasm of the host cell.

Such a connection implies that chlamydiae can inject proteins into the cytoplasm of the host cell. The apparatus may thus help chlamydiae resist interaction with lysosomes, because it can secrete proteins that remodel the vacuole membrane in ways that bar lysosome function. In addition, investigators have watched the chlamydiae-bearing vacuole divert artificially fluorescing lipids from certain compartments of the host cell, including the Golgi apparatus, to the vacuole membrane. Normally, the membrane of an entry vacuole bears molecules made by the pathogen inside. In this case, a membrane enclosing a bacterium would look foreign to the host cell, which would target the bacterium for immediate destruction by lysosomes. But the lipids that chlamydiae use to rebuild the membrane of their entry vacuole come from the host cell: the vacuoles are therefore indistinguishable from the host cell's organelles and invisible to lysosomes.

If scientists identify the proteins the bacteria secrete to camouflage vacuoles, they might be able to devise two kinds of infection-preventing treatments. One potential drug could interfere with the proteins' activity in a way that would force the entry vacuole to fuse with lysosomes, triggering an immune attack right after the chlamydiae invade the cell. Another drug might incapacitate the mechanisms the bacteria use to divert lipids from the host cell to the chlamydial vacuole, halting the trespassers' ability to hide. Hypothetically, such drugs could be incorporated into a topical microbicide that would thwart sexually transmitted chlamydiae.

Some of the proteins mentioned above—and any others that are unique to the bacteria and not made by human cells—might also be useful ingredients in vaccines. Newly sequenced genomes should be helpful in identifying good candidates.

Chlamydia's Stealthy Attack

Sexually transmitted chlamydia leaves most of its victims unaware of their infections until the damage is irreversible. In the worst case, infection of a woman's fallopian tubes creates scar tissue that stops a fertilized egg from reaching the uterus (*main illustration*), leading to a life-threatening tubal (ectopic) pregnancy. New revelations about the bacteria's survival tactics (*insets*) may soon make it possible to interrupt chlamydia's silent attack.

1 BACTERIA INVADE CELLS . . .
Sporelike forms of chlamydiae known as elementary bodies invade cells lining the genital tract by forming a pit on the cell surface (*below*). Enclosed within a pinched-off piece of the cell's outer membrane (known as an entry vacuole), elementary bodies begin differentiating into noninfectious reticulate bodies. The bacteria thrive by extracting nutrients from the host cells' cytoplasm.

Fallopian tube

Chlamydiae

Uterus

Elementary body

Entry vacuole

Reticulate body

Host cell cytoplasm

3 INFLAMMATION SETS IN
The body releases enzymes that dilate blood vessels and increase permeability across the vessel walls so that chlamydia-destroying immune cells and other molecules can migrate into the infected tissue. Some healthy tissue is destroyed in the process.

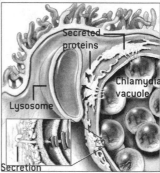

Secreted proteins

Chlamydia vacuole

Lysosome

Secretion apparatus

2 . . . AND WARD OFF HOST DEFENSES
Chlamydiae outsmart the host's defensive system by fending off lysosomes—constituents of the host cell that normally fuse with entry vacuoles harboring foreign intruders (*right*). Using a syringelike conduit known as a type III secretion apparatus, the bacteria may inject some of their own proteins into the outer membrane of the entry vacuole to physically block the lysosome's assault.

4 BACTERIA EVADE DETECTION . . .
Chlamydiae also hide from lysosomes, by refurbishing their entry vacuole with molecules they divert from the host cell's lipid distribution center, the Golgi apparatus (*below*). These stolen lipids make the vacuole virtually indistinguishable from the cell's own membrane-bound organelles.

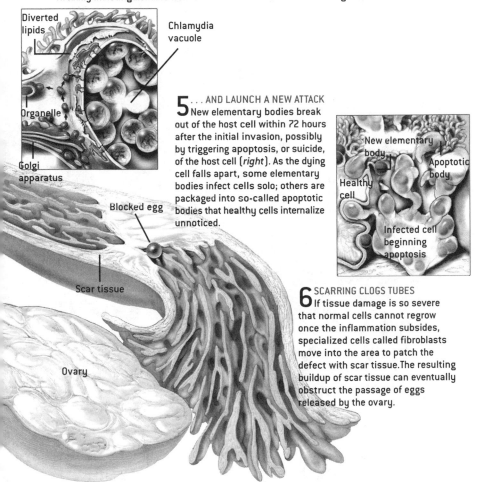

Diverted lipids

Chlamydia vacuole

Organelle

Golgi apparatus

Blocked egg

Scar tissue

Ovary

5 . . . AND LAUNCH A NEW ATTACK
New elementary bodies break out of the host cell within 72 hours after the initial invasion, possibly by triggering apoptosis, or suicide, of the host cell (*right*). As the dying cell falls apart, some elementary bodies infect cells solo; others are packaged into so-called apoptotic bodies that healthy cells internalize unnoticed.

New elementary body

Apoptotic body

Healthy cell

Infected cell beginning apoptosis

6 SCARRING CLOGS TUBES
If tissue damage is so severe that normal cells cannot regrow once the inflammation subsides, specialized cells called fibroblasts move into the area to patch the defect with scar tissue. The resulting buildup of scar tissue can eventually obstruct the passage of eggs released by the ovary.

Chlamydia, Interrupted

Sex education and improved hygiene cannot halt the spread of chlamydial infection on their own. That is why many scientists continue searching for an effective vaccine or other preventive treatments. Recent discoveries have suggested promising strategies, some listed below, for undermining the bacterium's survival tactics or limiting damage from an excessive immune response.

Kill the bacterium as it enters the body.
Develop a topical microbicide—a gel, cream or foam—that would be applied vaginally or rectally. Such products are in human trials to treat HIV, which infects the same tissues as chlamydia does.

Interfere with the bacterium's ability to invade the host cell.
Devise a vaccine that pumps up the host's antibody response. Following a vaccine or antibiotic treatment with anti-inflammatory drugs could decrease damage but has so far failed to do so in animal trials.

Inhibit the bacterium's growth within infected cells.
Interfere with the activity of the proteins chlamydia uses to divert lipids and other nutrients from the host cell. Such proteins have not yet been identified; once found, they could potentially be immobilized by a specially designed vaccine.

Promote intracellular destruction of the bacterium.
Disable the bacterium's type III secretion apparatus, which may release proteins that ward off lysosomes, constituents of the host cell that chop up foreign invaders.
In trials, bacteria with nearly identical apparatuses have been unable to cause symptoms of infection when scientists have disabled the genes that code for each apparatus; this finding suggests that drugs able to block the proteins encoded by those genes in chlamydia could be helpful.

Halt the bacterium's ability to spread.
Induce "suicide" of infected cells before the bacterium has a chance to convert into the form able to invade uninfected cells. Compounds that can induce premature cell death in tumors are under development; the same drugs could theoretically work against chlamydia.

Suicidal Tendencies

RECENT FINDINGS about the role of T cells may open
other doors. Biologists have long known that killer
T cells normally destroy infected cells by inducing a
type of cell death known as apoptosis or "cell suicide,"
during which cells use their own enzymes to lyse
their proteins and DNA. Also known is that immune
cells—including T cells and macrophages—stimulate
the production of cytokines that help to cripple bacteria
and to trigger an inflammatory response that stops
their spread. One cytokine known to have this dual
purpose is tumor necrosis factor-alpha (TNF-alpha).
Laboratory investigations have shown, however, that
some infected cells survive despite treatment with
TNF-alpha and other apoptosis-inducing cytokines,
leading to persistent infections. The problem is that
the body does not give up easily. Cytokines continue
to trigger chronic inflammation in an effort to
contain the infection even if they cannot eliminate it
outright.

But even persistently infected cells cannot live
forever. Indeed, it appears that chlamydiae have developed their own way to elicit the death of a host cell,
which they must do to ensure their own longevity.
(The host cell must fall apart before the bacteria can
infect other cells.) And as Jean-Luc Perfettini discovered
while working as a graduate student with one of us
(Ojcius) at the Pasteur Institute in Paris, chlamydiae can

kill and exit the infected cells in a way that minimizes
the host immune system's ability to sense any danger,
thereby allowing the infection to spread essentially
undetected in the body.

Addressing this final stage of the bacterial life
cycle will require further investigation into the proteins
involved in inducing apoptosis and in protecting persistently infected cells from suicidal signals. From
what biologists know so far, the latter avenue may prove
more fruitful in developing a vaccine. By rendering
persistently infected cells more sensitive to apoptosis,
it might be possible to eliminate the bacteria that
remain dormant in the system for long periods as
well as decrease the lasting consequences of chronic
infection.

Multiple Avenues of Attack

REGARDLESS OF THE DISCOVERIES that lie ahead, the
ideal chlamydia vaccine will not be a simple one. It
will have to activate both the antibody and cellular
arms of the immune system more effectively than the
body's natural response does yet somehow limit
inflammation as well. For those concerned with
preventing chlamydia-related STDs, an additional
challenge is ensuring that memory lymphocytes
remain in the genital tract poised to combat infection
at all times. This tract does not contain the type of
tissue that produces memory cells; such cells tend to

vacate the area, leaving the person susceptible to infection after a brief period of immunity.

Recall that females bear the lasting effects of genital infection. One feasible goal of a vaccine might be to protect women from the disease rather than from infection per se. This aim might be achieved by vaccinating both men and women. In this scenario, the vaccine would have to generate only enough antibodies to reduce, rather than eliminate, the amount of bacteria men carry. Then, if a woman were exposed to a man's infection through intercourse, memory cells induced by her immunization would travel to the genital tract in numbers adequate for killing the relatively small number of organisms before they spread to her fallopian tubes.

Until researchers manage to develop such a vaccine, contraceptives that include antichlamydial drugs could pay off. These agents might take the form of compounds that either block the proteins chlamydiae use to bind to genital tract cells or target the proteins the microbes secrete to promote intracellular survival. For eye infections, the only vaccine likely to be useful is one that completely prevents infection.

While awaiting effective preventive strategies against chlamydia, it is worth remembering that current antibiotic treatment is highly successful when it is accessible. New details from genomic discoveries indicate that this efficacy will continue. Compared with free-living bacterial pathogens, which can share genes easily, the genomes of Chlamydia species have remained essentially the same for millions of years. This genetic stability implies that chlamydiae cannot easily acquire genes—including those for antibiotic resistance—from other bacteria.

It is also worth noting that antibiotics cannot undo the tissue damage caused by inflammation, and to be most useful, they must be given early. Therefore, more widespread screening of high-risk individuals is needed. Researchers have already proved the feasibility of employing noninvasive urine screening of sexually active young men and women, particularly in settings such as high schools, military intake centers and juvenile detention facilities. Public health officials need to pursue such strategies in parallel with the ongoing search for effective vaccines.

More to Explore

Chlamydiae pneumoniae—An Infectious Risk Factor for Atherosclerosis? Lee Ann Campbell and Cho-cho Kuo in *Nature Reviews Microbiology*, Vol. 2, No. 1, pages 23–32; January 2004.

Chlamydia and Apoptosis: Life and Death Decisions of an Intracellular Pathogen. Gerald I. Byrne and David M. Ojcius in *Nature Reviews Microbiology*, Vol. 2, No. 10, pages 802–808; October 2004.

Basic information on the infections, genomes, basic biology and immunology of chlamydia can be found at **http://chlamydia-www.berkeley.edu:4231/** and **www.chlamydiae.com/chlamydiae/**

The Authors

DAVID M. OJCIUS, TONI DARVILLE and *PATRIK M. BAVOIL* each bring different expertise to chlamydia research. After studying the cellular and immunological aspects of infections for 12 years in France, Ojcius joined the faculty at the University of California, Merced, in 2004. Darville, who is a pediatric infectious disease specialist at the University of Arkansas for Medical Sciences, has explored the immunology of chlamydial infection since 1994 using mice and guinea pigs. As an associate professor at the University of Maryland, Baltimore, Bavoil works on the biochemistry and molecular biology of the disease.

"Attacking
3. Anthrax"

by John A. T. Young and R. John Collier

Recent discoveries are suggesting much-needed strategies
for improving prevention and treatment. High on the list:
ways to neutralize the anthrax bacterium's fiendish toxin

The need for new anthrax therapies became all too
clear last fall when five people died of inhalation
anthrax, victims of the first purposeful release of anthrax
spores in the U.S. Within days of showing initially
unalarming symptoms, the patients were gone, despite
intensive treatment with antibiotics. Six others became
seriously ill as well before pulling through.

Fortunately, our laboratories and others began
studying the causative bacterium, *Bacillus anthracis*,
and seeking antidotes long before fall 2001. Recent
findings are now pointing the way to novel medicines
and improved vaccines. Indeed, in the past year alone,
the two of us and our collaborators have reported on
three promising drug prototypes.

An Elusive Killer

THE NEW IDEAS for fighting anthrax have emerged from
ongoing research into how *B. anthracis* causes disease
and death. Anthrax does not spread from individual to
individual. A person (or animal) gets sick only after

incredibly hardy spores enter the body through a cut in the skin, through contaminated food or through spore-laden air. Inside the body the spores molt into "vegetative," or actively dividing, cells.

Anthrax bacteria that colonize the skin or digestive tract initially do damage locally and may cause self-limited ailments: black sores and swelling in the first instance; possibly vomiting and abdominal pain and bleeding in the second. If bacterial growth persists unchecked in the skin or gastrointestinal tract, however, the microbes may eventually invade the bloodstream and thereby cause systemic disease.

Inhaled spores that reach deep into the lungs tend to waste little time where they land. They typically convert to the vegetative form and travel quickly to lymph nodes in the middle of the chest, where many of the cells find ready access to the blood. (Meanwhile bacteria that remain in the chest set the stage for a breath-robbing buildup of fluid around the lungs.)

Extensive replication in the blood is generally what kills patients who succumb to anthrax. *B. anthracis*'s ability to expand so successfully derives from its secretion of two substances, known as virulence factors, that can profoundly derail the immune defenses meant to keep bacterial growth in check. One of these factors encases the vegetative cells in a polymer capsule that inhibits ingestion by the immune system's macrophages and neutrophils—the scavenger cells that normally degrade disease-causing bacteria. The capsule's partner in crime is an extraordinary toxin that works its way into those scavenger cells, or phagocytes, and interferes with their usual bacteria-killing actions.

The anthrax toxin, which also enters other cells, is thought to contribute to mortal illness not only by dampening immune responses but also by playing a direct role. Evidence for this view includes the observation that the toxin alone, in the absence of bacteria, can kill animals. Conversely, inducing the immune system to neutralize the toxin prevents *B. anthracis* from causing disease.

A Terrible Toxin

HARRY SMITH and his co-workers at the Microbiological Research Establishment in Wiltshire, England, discovered the toxin in the 1950s. Aware of its central part in anthrax's lethality, many researchers have since focused

Overview/Anthrax

- A three-part toxin produced by the anthrax bacterium, *Bacillus anthracis*, contributes profoundly to the symptoms and lethality of anthrax.
- The toxin causes trouble only when it gets into the cytosol of cells, the material that bathes the cell's internal compartments.
- Drugs that prevented the toxin from reaching the cytosol would probably go a long way toward limiting illness and saving the lives of people infected by the anthrax bacterium.
- Analyses of how the toxin enters cells have recently led to the discovery of several potential antitoxins.

on learning how the substance "intoxicates" cells—gets into them and disrupts their activities. Such details offer essential clues to blocking its effects. Stephen H. Leppla and Arthur M. Friedlander, while at the U.S. Army Medical Research Institute of Infectious Diseases, initiated that effort with their colleagues in the 1980s; the two of us and others took up the task somewhat later.

The toxin turns out to consist of three proteins: protective antigen, edema factor and lethal factor. These proteins cooperate but are not always joined together physically. They are harmless individually until they attach to and enter cells, which they accomplish in a highly orchestrated fashion.

First, protective antigen binds to the surface of a cell, where an enzyme trims off its outermost tip. Next, seven of those trimmed molecules combine to form a ring-shaped structure, or heptamer, that captures the two factors and is transported to an internal membrane-bound compartment called an endosome. Mild acidity in this compartment causes the heptamer to change shape in a way that leads to the transport of edema factor and lethal factor across the endosomal membrane into the cytosol (the internal matrix of cells), where they do their mischief. In essence, the heptamer is like a syringe loaded with edema factor and lethal factor, and the slight acidity of the endosome causes the syringe to pierce the membrane of the endosome and inject the toxic factors into the cytosol.

Edema factor and lethal factor catalyze different molecular reactions in cells. Edema factor upsets the controls on ion and water flow across cell membranes and thereby promotes the swelling of tissues. In phagocytes, it also saps energy that would otherwise be used to engulf bacteria.

The precise behavior of lethal factor, which could be more important in causing patient deaths, is less clear. Scientists do know that it is a protease (a protein-cutting enzyme) and that it cleaves enzymes in a family known as MAPKKs. Now they are trying to tease out the molecular events that follow such cleavage and to uncover the factor's specific contributions to disease and death.

Therapeutic Tactics

CERTAINLY DRUGS able to neutralize the anthrax toxin would help the immune system fight bacterial multiplication and would probably reduce a patient's risk of dying. At the moment, antibiotics given to victims of inhalation anthrax may control microbial expansion but leave the toxin free to wreak havoc.

In principle, toxin activity could be halted by interfering with any of the steps in the intoxication process. An attractive approach would stop the sequence almost before it starts, by preventing protective antigen from attaching to cells. Scientists realized almost 10 years ago that this protein initiated toxin entry by binding to some specific protein on the surface of cells; when cells were treated with enzymes that removed all their surface proteins, protective antigen found no footing.

Until very recently, though, no one knew which of the countless proteins on cells served as the crucial receptor.

The two of us, with our colleagues Kenneth Bradley, Jeremy Mogridge and Michael Mourez, found the receptor last summer. Detailed analysis of this molecule (now named ATR, for anthrax toxin receptor) then revealed that it spans the cell membrane and protrudes from it. The protruding part contains an area resembling a region that serves in other receptors as an attachment site for particular proteins. This discovery suggested that the area was the place where protective antigen latched onto ATR, and indeed it is.

We have not yet learned the normal function of the receptor, which surely did not evolve specifically to allow the anthrax toxin into cells. Nevertheless, knowledge of the molecule's makeup is enabling us to begin testing inhibitors of its activity. We have had success, for instance, with a compound called sATR, which is a soluble form of the receptor domain that binds to protective antigen. When sATR molecules are mixed into the medium surrounding cells, they serve as effective decoys, tricking protective antigen into binding to them instead of to its true receptor on cells.

We are now trying to produce sATR in the amounts needed for evaluating its ability to combat anthrax in rodents and nonhuman primates—experiments that must be done before any new drug can be considered for fighting anthrax in people. Other groups are examining whether carefully engineered antibodies (highly specific molecules of the immune system) might bind tightly to protective antigen in ways that will keep it from coupling with its receptor.

More Targets

SCIENTISTS ARE ALSO seeking ways to forestall later steps in the intoxication pathway. For example, a team from Harvard has constructed a drug able to clog the regions of the heptamer that grasp edema and lethal factors. The group—from the laboratories of one of us (Collier) and George M. Whitesides—reasoned that a plugged heptamer would be unable to draw the factors into cells.

We began by screening randomly constructed peptides (short chains of amino acids) to see if any of them bound to the heptamer. One did, so we examined its ability to block toxin activity. It worked, but weakly. Assuming that fitting many plugs into the heptamer's binding domains for edema and lethal factor would be more effective, we took advantage of chemical procedures devised by Whitesides's group and linked an average of 22 copies of the peptide to a flexible polymer. That construction showed itself to be a strong inhibitor of toxin action—more than 7,000 times better than the free peptide—both in cell cultures and in rats.

Another exciting agent, and the one probably closest to human testing, would alter the heptamer itself. This compound was discovered after Bret R. Sellman in Collier's group noted that when certain mutant forms of protective antigen were mixed with normal forms, the heptamers formed on cells as usual but were unable to inject edema and lethal factors into the cytosol. Remarkably, some of these mutants were so disruptive that a single copy in a heptamer completely prevented injection.

In a study reported last April, these mutants—known as dominant negative inhibitors, or DNIs—proved to be potent blockers of the anthrax toxin in cell cultures and in rats. Relatively small amounts of selected DNIs neutralized an amount of protective antigen and lethal factor that would otherwise kill a rat in 90 minutes. These findings suggest that each mutant copy of protective antigen is capable of inactivating six normal copies in the bloodstream and that it would probably reduce toxin activity in patients dramatically.

Of course, as more and more questions about the toxin are answered, scientists should discover further treatment ideas. Now that the receptor for protective antigen has been identified, researchers can use it as a target in screening tests aimed at finding drugs able to bar the receptor from binding to protective antigen. And understanding of the receptor's three-dimensional structure would reveal the precise contact points between protective antigen and the receptor, enabling drugmakers to custom-design receptor blocking agents.

Scientists would also like to uncover the molecular interactions that enable protective antigen heptamers to move from the cell surface into endosomes inside the cell. Impeding that migration should be very useful. And what happens after lethal factor cleaves MAPKK enzymes? How do those subsequent events affect cells?

Detecting Anthrax

Rapid sensing would save lives
by Rocco Casagrande

IF A TERRORIST GROUP spread anthrax spores into the open air, the release could affect large numbers of people but would probably go unnoticed until victims showed up at hospitals. Many would undoubtedly seek help too late to be saved by current therapies. Much illness could be prevented, however, if future defenses against anthrax attacks included sensors that raised an alarm soon after spores appeared in the environment. The needed instruments are not yet ready for deployment, but various designs that incorporate cutting-edge technology are being developed.

Environmental sensors must discriminate between disease-causing agents (pathogens) and the thousands of similar but harmless microorganisms that colonize air, water and soil. Most of the tools being investigated work by detecting unique molecules on the surface of the pathogens of interest or by picking out stretches of DNA found only in those organisms.

The Canary, which is being developed at the Massachusetts Institute of Technology Lincoln Laboratory, is an innovative example of the devices that detect pathogens based on unique surface molecules. The sensors of the Canary consist of living cells—B cells of the immune system—that have been genetically altered to emit light when their calcium levels change. Protruding from these cells are receptors that will bind only to a unique part of a surface molecule on a particular pathogen. When the cells in the sensor bind to their target, that binding triggers the release of calcium ions from stores within the cells, which in turn causes the cells to give off light. The Canary can discern more than one type of pathogen by running a sample through several cell-filled modules, each of which reacts to a selected microorganism.

The GeneXpert system, developed by Cepheid, in Sunnyvale, Calif., is an example of a gene-centered approach. It begins its work by extracting DNA from microorganisms in a sample. Then, if a pathogen of concern is present, small primers (strips of genetic material able to recognize specific short sequences of DNA) latch onto the ends of DNA fragments unique to the pathogen. Next, through a procedure called the polymerase chain reaction (PCR), the system makes many copies of the bound DNA, adding fluorescent labels to the new copies along the way. Within about 30 minutes GeneXpert can make enough DNA to reveal whether even a small amount of the worrisome organism inhabited the original sample.

This system contains multiple PCR reaction chambers with distinct primer sets to allow the detection of different pathogens simultaneously. Furthermore, the GeneXpert system could be used to determine whether the anthrax bacterium is present in a nasal swab taken from a patient in as little as half an hour, significantly faster than the time it takes for conventional microbiological techniques to yield results.

Instruments designed specifically to detect spores of the anthrax bacterium or of closely related microbes (such as the one that causes botulism) can exploit the fact that such spores are packed full of dipicolinic acid (DPA)—a compound, rarely found elsewhere in nature, that helps them to survive harsh environmental conditions. Molecules that fluoresce when bound to DPA have shown promise in chemically based anthrax detectors. "Electronic noses," such as the Cyranose detection system made by Cyrano Sciences in Pasadena, Calif., could possibly "smell" the presence of DPA in an air sample laced with anthrax spores.

The true danger of an anthrax release lies in its secrecy. If an attack is discovered soon after it occurs and if exposed individuals receive treatment promptly, victims have an excellent chance of surviving. By enhancing early detection, sensors based on the systems discussed above or on entirely different technologies could effectively remove a horrible weapon from a terrorist's arsenal.

ROCCO CASAGRANDE is a scientist at Surface Logix in Brighton, Mass., where he is developing methods and devices for detecting biological weapons.

Although the latter question remains a vexing challenge, recent study of lethal factor has brightened the prospects for finding drugs able to inactivate it. Last November, Robert C. Liddington of the Burnham Institute in La Jolla, Calif., and his colleagues in several laboratories published the three-dimensional structure of the part of lethal factor that acts on MAPKK molecules. That site can now become a target for drug screening or design.

New leads for drugs should also emerge from the recent sequencing of the code letters composing the *B. anthracis* genome. By finding genes that resemble those of known functions in other organisms, biologists are likely to discover additional information about how the anthrax bacterium causes disease and how to stop it.

Anthrax in Action

Physicians classify anthrax according to the tissues that are initially infected. The disease turns deadly when the causative bacterium, *Bacillus anthracis*, reaches the bloodstream and proliferates there, producing large amounts of a dangerous toxin. Much research is now focused on neutralizing the toxin.

THREE TYPES

INHALATION ANTHRAX
Spores are breathed in

GASTROINTESTINAL ANTHRAX
Spores are ingested by eating contaminated meat

CUTANEOUS ANTHRAX
Spores penetrate the skin through a break

HOW INHALATION ANTHRAX ARISES

Inhalation anthrax is the most dangerous form, probably because bacteria that land in the lungs are more likely to reach the bloodstream and thus disseminate their toxin through the body.

1 Immune system cells called macrophages ingest *B. anthracis* spores and carry them to lymph nodes in the chest. En route, or in the macrophages, the spores transform into actively dividing cells

2 Proliferating *B. anthracis* cells erupt from macrophages and infiltrate the blood readily

3 In the blood, the active bacteria evade destruction by macrophages and other cells of the immune system by producing a capsule (*detail*) that blocks the immune cells from ingesting them and by producing a toxin that enters immune cells and impairs their functioning

4 Protected from immune destruction, the bacteria multiply freely and spread through the body

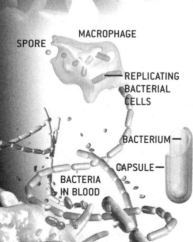

SPORE

MACROPHAGE

REPLICATING BACTERIAL CELLS

BACTERIUM

CAPSULE

BACTERIA IN BLOOD

MACROPHAGE FILLED WITH TOXIN

TOXIN MOLECULES

CELL

HOW THE TOXIN INVADES CELLS

THE ANTHRAX TOXIN must enter cells to hurt the body. It consists of three collaborating proteins: protective antigen (PA), edema factor (EF) and lethal factor (LF). The last two disrupt cellular activities, but only after protective antigen delivers them to the cytosol—the matrix surrounding the cell's intracellular compartments. Molecular understanding of how the factors reach the cytosol has led to ideas for blocking that journey and thus for neutralizing the toxin and saving lives.

LF

EF

HEPTAMER

4 Up to three copies of EF or LF or a combination of the two bind to the heptamer

3 Seven copies combine, forming a heptamer

PA

2 PA gets cleaved

ANTHRAX TOXIN RECEPTOR (ATR)

HEPTAMER COMPLEX

5 The heptamer complexed with EF and LF is delivered to a membrane-bound compartment called an endosome

1 PA binds to its receptor on a cell

ENDOSOME

6 Mild acidity in the endosome causes the heptamer to inject EF and LF into the cytosol

CYTOSOL

8 LF is believed to be important in causing disease and death, but exactly how it does so is in question

7 EF causes tissues to swell and prevents immune system cells from ingesting and degrading bacteria

The continuing research should yield several antitoxins. To be most effective, such drugs will probably be used with antibiotics, much as cocktails of antiviral drugs are recommended for treating HIV infection.

Promising Preventives

AS PLANS TO IMPROVE therapies proceed, so does work on better vaccines. Vaccines against toxin-producing bacteria often prime the immune system to neutralize the toxin of concern as soon as it appears in the body, thus preventing disease. Livestock in parts of the U.S. receive preparations consisting of *B. anthracis* cells that lack the protective capsule and thus replicate poorly. A similar vaccine for humans has been used in the former Soviet Union. But preparations that contain whole microbes often cause side effects, and they raise the specter that renegade cells might at times give rise to the very diseases they were meant to prevent.

The only anthrax vaccine approved for human use in the U.S. takes a different form. It consists primarily of toxin molecules that have been chemically treated to prevent them from making people ill. It is produced by growing the weakened strain of *B. anthracis* in culture, filtering the bacterial cells from the culture medium, adsorbing the toxin proteins in the remaining filtrate onto an adjuvant (a substance that enhances immune responses) and treating the mixture with formaldehyde to inactivate the proteins. Injection of this preparation, known as AVA (for anthrax vaccine adsorbed), stimulates the immune system to produce

---

Medical Lessons

Doctors now have a changed view of inhalation anthrax
by Ricki L. Rusting

THE RECENT CASES of inhalation anthrax in the U.S. have upended some old assumptions about that disease. When contaminated letters started appearing in September 2001, public health authorities initially believed that only those who received the letters, and perhaps individuals nearby, were in danger. But spores clearly seeped out through the weave of the envelopes, contaminating postal facilities and jumping to other mail. Such "cross contamination" is a leading explanation for the deaths of two of the 11 people confirmed to have contracted inhalation anthrax last year. Also contrary to expectations, spores do not remain sedentary once they land. They can become airborne again as people walk around in a tainted room.

One surprise was positive. Before October 2001 common wisdom held that inhalation anthrax was almost always incurable after symptoms appeared. But doctors beat those odds last fall, saving six of the victims. What made the difference? Researchers cannot draw firm conclusions from so few cases. But some intriguing patterns emerged when John A. Jernigan of the Centers for Disease Control and Prevention (CDC) and a team of others reviewed the medical records of the first 10 patients. Their findings appear in the November/December 2001 *Emerging Infectious Diseases* and online at www.cdc.gov/ncidod/eid/vol7no6/jernigan.htm

Relatively prompt diagnosis may have helped, the researchers report. Inhalation anthrax has two symptomatic phases—an early period marked by maladies common to a variety of ailments (such as fatigue, fever, aches and cough) and a later phase in which patients become critically ill with high fever, labored breathing and shock. Six of the 10 patients received antibiotics active against the anthrax bacterium, *Bacillus anthracis*, while they were still showing early symptoms of infection, and only they survived.

The types of antibiotics prescribed and the use of combinations of drugs might also have had a hand in the unexpectedly high survival rate. Nine of the people discussed in the review sought care before the CDC published what it called "interim" guidelines for treating inhalation anthrax on October 26, but most patients received therapy consistent with those guidelines: ciprofloxacin (the now famous Cipro) or doxycycline plus one or two other agents known to inhibit replication of *B. anthracis* (such as rifampin, vancomycin, penicillin, ampicillin, chloramphenicol, imipenem, clindamycin and clarithromycin). Aggressive "supportive" care—including draining dangerous fluid from around the lungs—probably helped as well, scientists say.

Even the survivors were very sick, however. Jernigan says they are still being observed to see whether long-term complications will develop, although as of mid-January no obvious signs of such problems had emerged. Researchers suspect that anthrax antitoxins would ease the course of many people afflicted with anthrax and might also rescue patients who could not be saved with current therapies.

Ricki L. Rusting is a staff editor and writer.

antibodies that specifically bind to and inactivate the toxin's components. Most of the antibodies act on protective antigen, however, which explains the protein's name: it is the component that best elicits protective immunity.

AVA is given to soldiers and certain civilians but is problematic as a tool for shielding the general public against biological warfare. Supplies are limited. And even if AVA were available in abundance, it would be cumbersome to deliver on a large scale; the standard protocol calls for six shots delivered over 18 months followed by annual boosters. The vaccine has not been licensed for use in people already exposed to anthrax spores. But late last year officials, worried that spores might sometimes survive in the lungs for a long time, began offering an abbreviated, three-course dose on an experimental basis to postal workers and others who had already taken 60 days of precautionary antibiotics. People who accepted the offer were obliged to take antibiotics for an additional 40 days, after which the immunity stimulated by the vaccine would presumably be strong enough to provide adequate protection on its own.

In hopes of producing a more powerful, less cumbersome and faster-acting vaccine, many investigators are focusing on developing inoculants composed primarily of protective antigen produced by recombinant DNA technology. By coupling the recombinant protein with a potent new-generation adjuvant, scientists may be able to evoke good protective immunity relatively quickly with only one or two injections. The dominant negative inhibitors discussed earlier as possible treatments could be useful forms of protective antigen to choose. Those molecules retain their ability to elicit immune responses. Hence, they could do double duty: disarming the anthrax toxin in the short run while building up immunity that will persist later on.

We have no doubt that the expanding research on the biology of B. *anthracis* and on possible therapies and vaccines will one day provide a range of effective anthrax treatments. We fervently hope that these efforts will mean that nobody will have to die from anthrax acquired either naturally or as a result of biological terrorism.

More to Explore

Anthrax as a Biological Weapon: Medical and Public Health Management. Thomas V. Inglesby et al. in *Journal of the American Medical Association*, Vol. 281, No. 18, pages 1735–1745; May 12, 1999.

Dominant-Negative Mutants of a Toxin Subunit: An Approach to Therapy of Anthrax. Bret R. Sellman, Michael Mourez and R. John Collier in *Science*, Vol. 292, pages 695–697; April 27, 2001.

Designing a Polyvalent Inhibitor of Anthrax Toxin. Michael Mourez et al. in *Nature Biotechnology*, Vol. 19, pages 958–961; October 2001.

Identification of the Cellular Receptor for Anthrax Toxin. Kenneth A. Bradley, Jeremy Mogridge,

Michael Mourez, R. John Collier and John
A. T. Young in *Nature*, Vol. 414, pages 225–229;
November 8, 2001.
The U.S. Centers for Disease Control and Prevention
maintain a Web site devoted to anthrax at **www.
cdc.gov/ncidod/dbmd/diseaseinfo/anthrax_g.htm**

The Authors

JOHN A. T. YOUNG and *R. JOHN COLLIER* have
collaborated for several years on investigating the
anthrax toxin. Young is Howard M. Temin Professor of
Cancer Research in the McArdle Laboratory for Cancer
Research at the University of Wisconsin–Madison.
Collier, who has studied anthrax for more than 14 years,
is Maude and Lillian Presley Professor of Microbiology
and Molecular Genetics at Harvard Medical School.

4. "Detecting Mad Cow Disease"

by Stanley B. Prusiner

New tests can rapidly identify the presence of dangerous prions—the agents responsible for the malady—and several compounds offer hope for treatment

Last December mad cow disease made its U.S. debut when federal officials announced that a holstein from Mabton, Wash., had been stricken with what is formally known as bovine spongiform encephalopathy (BSE). The news kept scientists, government officials, the cattle industry and the media scrambling for information well past New Year's. Yet the discovery of the sick animal came as no surprise to many of us who study mad cow disease and related fatal disorders that devastate the brain. The strange nature of the prion—the pathogen at the root of these conditions—made us realize long ago that controlling these illnesses and ensuring the safety of the food supply would be difficult.

As researchers learn more about the challenges posed by prions—which can incubate without symptoms for years, even decades—they uncover strategies that could better forestall epidemics. Key among these tools are highly sensitive tests, some available and some under development, that can detect prions even in asymptomatic individuals; currently BSE is diagnosed only after an animal has died naturally or been slaughtered. Researchers have also made some headway in treating a human prion disorder called Creutzfeldt-Jakob disease (CJD), which today is uniformly fatal.

Identifying the Cause

ALTHOUGH MASS CONCERN over mad cow disease is new in the U.S., scientific efforts to understand and combat it and related disorders began heating up some time ago. In the early 1980s I proposed that the infectious pathogen causing scrapie (the sheep analogue of BSE) and CJD consists only of a protein, which I termed the prion. The prion theory was greeted with great skepticism in most quarters and with outright disdain in others, as it ran counter to the conventional wisdom that pathogens capable of reproducing must contain DNA or RNA [see "Prions," by Stanley B. Prusiner; SCIENTIFIC AMERICAN, October 1984]. The doubt I encountered was healthy and important, because most dramatically novel ideas are eventually shown to be incorrect. Nevertheless, the prion concept prevailed.

In the years since my proposal, investigators have made substantial progress in deciphering this fascinating protein. We know that in addition to causing scrapie and CJD, prions cause other spongiform encephalopathies, including BSE and chronic wasting disease in deer and elk [see "The Prion Diseases," by Stanley B. Prusiner; SCIENTIFIC AMERICAN, January 1995]. But perhaps the most startling finding has been that the prion protein, or PrP, is not always bad. In fact, all animals studied so far have a gene that codes for PrP. The normal form of the protein, now called PrP^C (C for cellular), appears predominantly in nerve cells and may help maintain neuronal functioning. But the protein can twist into an abnormal, disease-causing shape, denoted PrP^{Sc} (Sc for scrapie, the prion disease that until recently was the most studied).

Unlike the normal version, PrP^{Sc} tends to form difficult-to-dissolve clumps that resist heat, radiation and chemicals that would kill other pathogens. A few minutes of boiling wipes out bacteria, viruses and molds, but not PrP^{Sc}. This molecule makes more of itself by converting normal prion proteins into abnormal forms: PrP^{Sc} can induce PrP^C to refold and become PrP^{Sc}. Cells have the ability to break down and eliminate misfolded proteins, but if they have difficulty clearing PrP^{Sc} faster than it forms, PrP^{Sc} builds up, ruptures cells and creates the characteristic pathology of these diseases—namely, masses of protein and microscopic holes in the brain, which begins to resemble a sponge. Disease symptoms appear as a result.

Prion diseases can afflict people and animals in various ways. Most often the diseases are "sporadic"— that is, they happen spontaneously for no apparent reason. Sporadic CJD is the most common prion disease among humans, striking approximately one in a million, mostly older, people. Prion diseases may also result from a mutation in the gene that codes for the prion protein; many families are known to pass on CJD and two other disorders, Gerstmann-Sträussler-Scheinker disease and fatal insomnia. To date, researchers have uncovered more than 30 different mutations in the PrP gene that lead to the hereditary forms of the sickness— all of which are rare, occurring about once in every 10 million people. Finally, prion disease may result from an infection, through, for instance, the consumption of bovine prions.

Tracing the Mad Cow Epidemic

THE WORLD AWOKE to the dangers of prion disease in cows after the BSE outbreak that began ravaging the British beef industry in the mid-1980s. The truly novel concepts emerging from prion science forced researchers and society to think in unusual ways and made coping with the epidemic difficult. Investigators eventually learned that prions were being transmitted to cattle through meat-and-bone meal, a dietary supplement prepared from the parts of sheep, cattle, pigs and chickens that are processed, or rendered, for industrial use. High heat eliminated conventional pathogens, but PrP^{Sc} survived and went on to infect cattle.

As infected cattle became food for other cattle, BSE began appearing throughout the U.K. cattle population, reaching a high of 37,280 identified cases in 1992. The British authorities instituted some feed bans beginning in 1989, but it was not until 1996 that a strict ban on cannibalistic feeding finally brought BSE under control

A Bad Influence

Prion proteins exist in at least two forms (*below*)—the normal, or cellular, version (PrP^C) and the disease-causing one (PrP^Sc). In a process that is not well understood, PrP^Sc changes PrP^C into more PrP^Sc; the newly altered prions, in turn, can corrupt other normal ones (*bottom*). Usually the body eliminates PrP^Sc before too much of it accumulates. But if it does build up and is not successfully removed by the cell's machinery, illness can result.

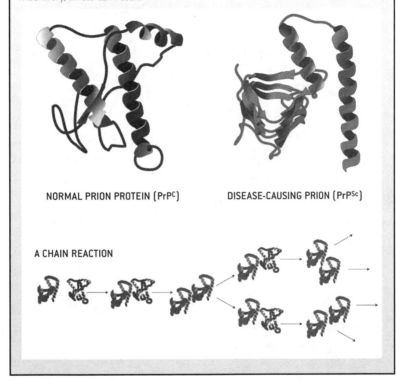

NORMAL PRION PROTEIN (PrP^C)   **DISEASE-CAUSING PRION (PrP^Sc)**

A CHAIN REACTION

in the U.K.; the country saw 612 cases last year. Overall the U.K. has identified about 180,000 mad cows, and epidemiological models suggest that another 1.9 million were infected but undetected.

For many people, the regulations came too late. Despite the British government's early assurances to the contrary, mad cow disease proved transmissible to humans. In March 1996 Robert Will, James Ironside and Jeanne Bell, who were working in the National CJD Surveillance Unit in Edinburgh, reported that 11 British teenagers and young adults had died of a variant of Creutzfeldt-Jakob disease (vCJD). In these young patients the patterns of PrP^{Sc} deposition in the brain differed markedly from that found in typical CJD patients.

Many scientists, including myself, were initially dubious of the presumed link between BSE and vCJD. I eventually changed my mind, under the weight of many studies. One of these was conducted by my colleagues at the University of California at San Francisco, Michael Scott and Stephen DeArmond, who collected data in mice genetically engineered to resemble cattle,

Overview/Rooting Out Prions

- The recent discoveries of cows afflicted with mad cow disease, or bovine spongiform encephalopathy (BSE), in the U.S., Canada and elsewhere emphasize the need for better tests and policies so that infection does not spread and the public is reassured.
- Several new tests make such identification much more rapid than it has been, and some are able to identify low levels of dangerous prions so officials will not have to wait until cattle are sick before they know there is a problem.
- Invention of a blood test would allow diagnoses to be made for living animals and for people and could be important if some of the therapies now being investigated to treat prion diseases in humans prove to be effective.

at least from a prion protein point of view (the PrP gene from cattle was inserted into the mouse genome). These mice became ill approximately nine months after receiving injections of prions from cattle with BSE or people with vCJD, and the resulting disease looked the same whether the prions originated from cows or vCJD patients.

As of February 2004, 146 people have been diagnosed with vCJD in the U.K. and another 10 elsewhere. No one knows exactly how many other people are incubating prions that cause vCJD. Epidemiological models suggest that only a few dozen more individuals will develop vCJD, but these models are based on assumptions that may prove wrong. One assumption, for example, is that vCJD affects only those with a particular genetic makeup. Because prions incubate for so long, it will take some time before we know the ultimate number of vCJD cases and whether they share similar genetics.

In vCJD, PrPSc builds up, not just in the brain but also in the lymphoid system, such as the tonsils and appendix, suggesting that PrPSc enters the bloodstream at some point. Animal studies have shown that prions can be transmitted to healthy animals through blood transfusions from infected animals. In response to this information, many nations have enacted stricter blood donation rules. In the U.K., people born after 1996, when the tough feed ban came into force, can receive blood only from overseas (those born before are considered already exposed). In the U.S., those who spent three months or more in the U.K. between 1980 and 1996 cannot give blood.

Although such restrictions have contributed to periodic blood shortages, the measures appear justified. Last December the U.K. announced the vCJD death of one of 15 individuals who received transfusions from donors who later developed vCJD. The victim received the transfusion seven and a half years before his death. It is possible that he became infected through prion-tainted food, but his age argues against that: at 69, he was much older than the 29 years of typical vCJD patients. Thus, it seems fairly likely that vCJD is not limited to those who have eaten prion-infected beef.

Since the detection of mad cow disease in the U.K., two dozen other nations have uncovered cases. Canada and the U.S. are the latest entrants. On May 20, 2003, Canadian officials reported BSE in an eight-and-a-half-year-old cow that had spent its life in Alberta and Saskatchewan. (The country's only previous mad cow had arrived as a U.K. import 10 years earlier.) Although the animal had been slaughtered in January 2003, slow processing meant that officials did not test the cow remains until April. By then, the carcass had been turned into pet food exported to the U.S.

Seven months later, on December 23, the U.S. Department of Agriculture announced the country's first case of BSE, in Washington State. The six-and-a-half-year-old dairy cow had entered the U.S. at the age of four. The discovery means that U.S. officials can no longer labor under the misconception that the nation is free of BSE. Like Canada, U.S. agricultural interests want the BSE problem to disappear. Financial woes stem primarily from reduced beef exports: 58 other countries are keeping their borders shut, and a $3-billion export market has largely evaporated.

Designing Diagnostics

THE MOST straightforward way to provide this assurance—both for foreign nations and at home—appears to be simple: just test the animals being slaughtered for food and then stop the infected ones from entering the food supply, where they could transmit

A Worldview

Many countries have reported cattle afflicted with BSE, but cases of human infection thought to stem from eating meat from sick cows—variant Creutzfeldt-Jakob disease (vCJD)—remain low, for now at least.

COUNTRY	BSE CASES	vCJD DEATHS (current cases)
Austria	1	0
Belgium	125	0
Canada	2	1
Czech Republic	9	0
Denmark	13	0
Falkland Islands	1	0
Finland	1	0
France	891	6
Germany	312	0
Greece	1	0
Hong Kong	0	1*
Ireland	1,353	1
Israel	1	0
Italy	117	1
Japan	11	0
Lichtenstein	2	0
Luxembourg	2	0
Netherlands	75	0
Oman	2	0
Poland	14	0
Portugal	875	0
Slovakia	15	0
Slovenia	4	0
Spain	412	0
Switzerland	453	0
U.S.	1	0 (1)[†]
U.K.	183,803	141 (5)
Worldwide		151(6)

*Awaiting confirmation   [†]British subject

Testing for Mad Cow

Four kinds of tests are now used to detect dangerous prions (PrP^{Sc}) in brain tissue from dead cattle. By identifying infected animals, public health officials and farmers can remove them from the food supply. Some of these tests, however, are time-consuming and expensive, so researchers are working to develop the ideal diagnostic: one that could quickly detect even tiny amounts of PrP^{Sc} in blood and urine and thus could work for live animals and people. The hope is to forestall outbreaks by catching infection as early as possible and, eventually, to treat infection before it progresses to disease.

BIOASSAY

The bioassay can take up to 36 months to provide results and can be very expensive. Its advantage is that it can reveal particular strains of prions as well as how infectious the sample is based on the time it takes for the test animal to become sick.

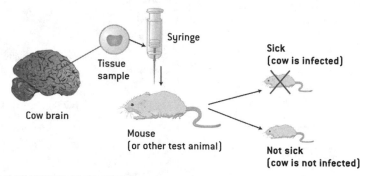

IMMUNOHISTOCHEMISTRY

The first test used to specifically detect prions, immunohistochemistry is considered the gold standard that other tests must meet. But because technicians must examine each slide, the process is very time-consuming, often taking as many as seven days, and is not useful for mass screenings.

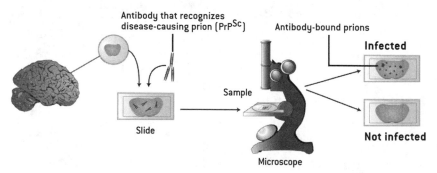

IMMUNOASSAY

Many companies produce immunoassays, and these rapid tests are now in widespread use in Europe; they have just been introduced to the U.S. Results can be had within eight hours, and hundreds of samples can be run simultaneously. These tests work well only with high levels of PrP^{Sc}.

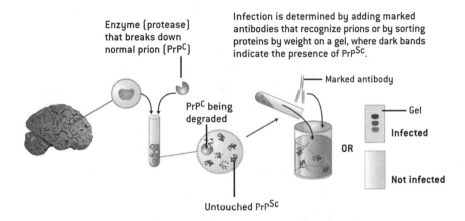

Enzyme (protease) that breaks down normal prion (PrP^C)

Infection is determined by adding marked antibodies that recognize prions or by sorting proteins by weight on a gel, where dark bands indicate the presence of PrP^{Sc}.

Marked antibody

PrP^C being degraded

Gel

OR

Infected

Not infected

Untouched PrP^{Sc}

CONFORMATION-DEPENDENT IMMUNOASSAY (CDI)

This automated test can detect very low levels of PrP^{Sc} and reveal how much of the dangerous prion is present in the sample without first having to degrade PrP^C. It informs experts about the animal's level of infection within five hours or so. It has been approved for testing in Europe. CDI is being tested on tissue from live animals and might one day serve as a blood test.

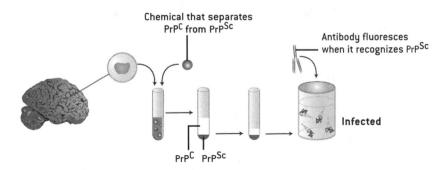

Chemical that separates PrP^C from PrP^{Sc}

Antibody fluoresces when it recognizes PrP^{Sc}

Infected

PrP^C PrP^{Sc}

pathogenic prions to humans. But testing is not easy. The USDA uses immunohistochemistry, an old technique that is cumbersome and extremely time-consuming (taking a few days to complete) and so is impractical for universal application.

Accordingly, others and I have been working on alternatives. In the mid-1980s researchers at my lab and elsewhere produced new kinds of antibodies that can help identify dangerous prions in the brain more efficiently. These antibodies, similar to those used in the standard test, recognize any prion—normal or otherwise. To detect PrP^{Sc}, we need to first remove any trace of PrP^{C}, which is done by applying a protease (protein-degrading enzyme) to a brain sample. Because PrP^{Sc} is generally resistant to the actions of proteases, much of it remains intact. Antibodies then added to the sample will reveal the amount of PrP^{Sc} present. Using a similar approach, a handful of companies, including Prionics in Switzerland and Bio-Rad in France, have developed their own antibodies and commercial kits. The results can be obtained in a few hours, which is why such kits are proving useful in the mass screenings under way in Europe and Japan. (Japan discovered its first case of BSE in 2001 and by this past April had reported 11 infected cows in total.)

These rapid tests, however, have limitations. They depend on PrP^{Sc} accumulating to detectable amounts— quite often, relatively high levels—in an animal's brain. Yet because BSE often takes three to five years to develop, most slaughter-age cattle, which tend to be younger than two years, usually do not test positive, even if they are infected. Therefore, these tests are generally most reliable for older bovines, regardless of whether they look healthy or are "downers." At the moment, downer cattle, which cannot stand on their own, are the group most likely to be tested.

Until new regulations came out in January, the U.S. annually sent roughly 200,000 downers to slaughter for human consumption. Of these, only a fraction were tested. Over the next year, however, the USDA will examine at least 200,000 cows for BSE. (Whether milk can be affected remains open; my laboratory is testing milk from BSE-infected cattle.)

Because of the limitations of the existing tests, developing one that is able to detect prions in the bulk of the beef supply—that is, in asymptomatic young animals destined for slaughter—continues to be one of the most important weapons in confronting prion disease outbreaks.

Scientists have pursued several strategies. One tries to boost the amount of PrP^{Sc} in a sample so the prions are less likely to escape detection. If such an amplification system can be created, it might prove useful in developing a blood test for use in place of ones that require an animal's sacrifice (not enough PrP^{Sc} circulates in the blood to be detectable by current methods). Claudio Soto of Serono Pharmaceuticals and his colleagues have attempted to carry this out. They mixed brain preparations from normal and scrapie-infected hamsters and then subjected the mixture to sound pulses to break apart clumps of PrP^{Sc} so it could convert the normal form of the prion protein into the rogue version. The experiment resulted in a

Spontaneous Prion Disease

Because prion diseases have aspects that resemble those caused by viruses, many people use viral analogies when talking about prions. But these analogies can sow confusion. An example is the presumed origin of the mad cows in Canada and the U.S. Although it is true that bovine spongiform encephalopathy (BSE) first appeared in the U.K. and then spread elsewhere through exported prion-contaminated feed, the idea of a traditional bacterial or viral epidemic is only partly helpful. In those situations, quarantines or bans can curb the spread of disease. But prions can arise spontaneously, which is an extremely important characteristic that distinguishes prions from viruses. In fact, any mammal is capable of producing prions spontaneously.

Spontaneous prion disease, for instance, is thought to have triggered the epidemic of kuru, which decimated a group called the Fore in New Guinea in the past century. The theory is that Creutzfeldt-Jakob disease occurred in an individual, whose brain was then consumed by his or her fellow Fore in a funerary rite involving cannibalism. The continued practice created a kuru epidemic.

Similarly, a feed ban that prevents cows from eating the remains of other animals is crucial in containing BSE. But such bans will not eliminate the presence of mad cows when pathogenic prions arise spontaneously. If every year one out of a million humans spontaneously develops a prion disease, why not the same for cows? Indeed, I suspect that the North American BSE cases could well have arisen spontaneously and that afflicted animals have occasionally appeared unrecognized in herds ever since humans started cattle ranching. We have been extraordinarily lucky that a past spontaneous case did not trigger an American BSE epidemic. Or perhaps small epidemics did happen but went undetected.

Still, many prefer the idea that the two mad cows in North America acquired prions from their feed. Such reasoning allows people to equate prions with viruses—that is, to think of prions only as infectious agents (even though they can also be inherited and occur spontaneously)—and to offer a seemingly plausible plan to eradicate BSE by quarantining herds. But ignoring the revolutionary concepts that govern prion biology can only hamper efforts at developing an effective program to protect the American public from exposure to these deadly agents. We must think beyond quarantine and bans and test for prions even in the absence of an epidemic. —S. B. P.

10-fold increase in protease-resistant prion protein. Surachai Supattapone of Dartmouth Medical School has obtained similar results.

Another strategy focuses on the intricacies of the protein shape instead of trying to bolster amounts. A test I developed with my U.C.S.F. colleague Jiri Safar, for example, is based on the ability of some antibodies to react with either PrP^C or PrP^{Sc}, but not both. Specifically, the antibody targets a portion of the prion protein that is accessible in one conformation but that is tucked away in the alternative conformation, much like a fitted corner of a sheet is hidden when folded. This specificity means that test samples do not have to be subjected to proteases. Removing the protease step is important because we now know that a form of PrP^{Sc} is sensitive to the action of proteases, which means that tests that eliminate PrP^C probably also eliminate most or all of the protease-sensitive PrP^{Sc}— and so these tests could well underestimate the amount of PrP^{Sc} present by as much as 90 percent.

Our test—the conformation-dependent immunoassay (CDI)—gained approval for use in Europe in 2003 and might be sensitive enough to detect PrP^{Sc} in blood. The CDI has already shown promise in screening young cows. In the fall of 2003 Japan reported two cases of BSE in cows 21 and 23 months of age. Neither animal showed outward signs of neurological dysfunction. In the case of the 23-month-old cow, two commercially available tests for PrP^{Sc} returned inconclusive, borderline-positive results, but the CDI showed that the brain stem harbored malevolent prions.

Neither of these cases would have been discovered in Europe, where only cattle older than 30 months (24 months in Germany) must be tested if they are destined for human consumption. Initially the Japanese government proposed adopting the European Union's testing protocol. But consumer advocates forced the government to change its policy and test every slaughtered animal. Given that seemingly healthy animals can potentially carry pathogenic prions, I believe that testing all slaughtered animals is the only rational policy. Until now, the tests have been inadequately sensitive. But the advent of rapid, sensitive tests means universal screening can become the norm. (I understand that this statement could seem self-serving because I have a financial interest in the company making the CDI test. But I see no other option for adequately protecting the human food supply.)

Some New Insights

DURING OUR WORK on the CDI, we discovered a surprising fact about the development of prion disease. As alluded to above, we found that the prion is actually a collection of proteins having different degrees of resistance to protease digestion. We also learned that protease-sensitive forms of PrP^{Sc} appear long before the protease-resistant forms appear. Whether protease-sensitive PrP^{Sc} is an intermediate in the formation of protease-resistant PrP^{Sc} remains to be determined. Regardless, a test that could identify

The Significance of Strains

One distinct characteristic that prions do share with viruses is variability; they can come in strains—forms that behave somewhat differently. Laboratory work convincingly shows that prion strains result from different conformations of PrPSc, but no one has yet figured out exactly how the structure of a given strain influences its particular biological properties. Nevertheless, strains can clearly cause different illnesses. In humans, Creutzfeldt-Jakob disease, kuru, fatal insomnia and Gerstmann-Sträussler-Scheinker disease all result from different strains. Sheep have as many as 20 kinds of scrapie. And BSE may also come in various versions. For instance, a 23-month-old animal in Japan and another cow in Slovakia had a good deal of PrPSc in the midbrain, whereas in most cases PrPSc tends to accumulate in the brain stem.

The necessity of recognizing and understanding strains has become clear in studies of sheep exposed to BSE prions. A particular breed of sheep, called the ARR/ARR genotype, resists scrapie, the ovine form of mad cow disease (the letters refer to amino acids on the sheep's prion protein). And so several European countries have created scrapie eradication programs based on breeding flocks with the ARR/ARR genotype. Yet these sheep get sick when inoculated with BSE prions. That these sheep are resistant to scrapie but susceptible to BSE prions has important implications for farming practices. It can be argued that such homogeneous populations will only serve to increase the incidence of BSE prions in sheep. Such a situation could prove to be dangerous to humans who consume lamb and mutton because scrapie strains do not seem to sicken humans, whereas BSE prions do. Experiments with animals should be conducted to see if BSE prions from sheep are as deadly as those from cows before livestock experts continue with selective sheep-breeding programs. —S. B. P.

protease-sensitive forms should be able to detect infection before symptoms appear, so the food supply can have maximum protection and infected patients can be assisted as early as possible. Fortunately, by using the CDI, my colleagues and I have been able to detect low levels of the protease-sensitive forms of PrPSc in the blood of rodents and humans.

Hunting for prions in blood led us to another surprise as well. Patrick Bosque, now at the University of Colorado's Health Sciences Center, and I found prions in the hind limb muscles of mice at a level 100,000 times as high as that found in blood; other muscle groups had them, too, but at much lower levels. Michael Beekes and his colleagues at the Robert Koch Institute in Berlin discovered PrP^{Sc} in virtually all muscles after they fed prions to their hamsters, although they report high levels of prions in all muscles, not just in the hind limbs. (We do not know why our results differ or why the hind limbs might be more prone to supporting prions than other muscles are.) These findings were not observed in rodents exclusively but in human patients as well. U.C.S.F. scientists Safar and DeArmond found PrP^{Sc} in the muscles of some CJD patients, and Adriano Aguzzi and his colleagues at the University of Zurich identified PrP^{Sc} in the muscles of 25 percent of the CJD patients they examined.

Of course, the ideal way to test for prions would be a noninvasive method, such as a urine test. Unfortunately, so far the only promising lead—discovery of protease-resistant PrP in urine—could not be confirmed in later studies.

Novel Therapies

ALTHOUGH NEW diagnostics will improve the safety of the food and blood supply, they will undoubtedly distress people who learn that they have a fatal disease. Therefore, many investigators are looking at ways to block prion formation or to boost a cell's ability to clear existing prions. So far researchers have identified more than 20 compounds that can either inhibit prion formation or enhance prion clearance in cultured cells. Several compounds have been shown to extend the lives of mice or hamsters when administered around the time they were inoculated with prions, but none have been shown to alter the course of disease when administered well after the initial infection occurred. Furthermore, many of these agents require high doses to exert their effects, suggesting that they would be toxic in animals.

Beyond the problem of potential toxicity that high doses might entail lies the challenge of finding drugs that can cross the blood-brain barrier and travel from the bloodstream into brain tissue. Carsten Korth, now at Heinrich Heine University in Dusseldorf, and I—and, independently, Katsumi Doh-ura of Kyushu University in Japan and Byron Caughey of the National Institute of Allergy and Infectious Diseases—have found that certain drugs known to act in the brain, such as thorazine (used in the treatment of schizophrenia), inhibit prion formation in cultured cells. Another compound, quinacrine, an antimalarial drug with a structure that resembles thorazine, is approximately 10 times as powerful.

Quinacrine has shown some efficacy in animals. My co-workers and I administered quinacrine to mice, starting 60 days after we injected prions into their brain, and found that the incubation time (from the moment of infection to the manifestation of disease) was prolonged nearly 20 percent compared with untreated animals. Such an extension might be quite significant for humans with prion diseases if they could be made to tolerate the high levels of quinacrine needed or if more potent relatives of the drug could be made. My U.C.S.F. colleagues Barnaby May and Fred E. Cohen are pursuing the potency problem. In cell cultures, they have boosted the effectiveness of quinacrine 10-fold by joining two of its molecules together.

Another therapeutic approach involves the use of antibodies that inhibit PrP^{Sc} formation in cultured cells. Several teams have had some success using this strategy. In mice inoculated with prions in the gut and then given antibodies directed against prion proteins, the incubation period was prolonged. So far, however, only a few patients have received antiprion drugs. Quinacrine has been administered orally to patients with vCJD and to individuals who have the sporadic or genetic forms of prion disease. It has not cured them, but it may have slowed the progression of disease; we await further evidence.

Physicians have also administered pentosan poly-sulfate to vCJD patients. Generally prescribed to treat a bladder condition, the molecule is highly charged and is unlikely to cross the blood-brain barrier, so it has been injected directly into a ventricle of the brain. The drug has apparently slowed the progression of vCJD in one young man, but it seems unlikely that it will diffuse throughout the brain because similarly charged drugs—administered in the same way—have not.

A controlled clinical trial is needed before any assessment of efficacy can be made for quinacrine and other antiprion drugs. Even an initial clinical trial may prove to be insufficient because we have no information about how delivery of the drug should be scheduled. For example, many cancer drugs must be given episodically, where the patient alternates periods on and off the drug, to minimize toxicity.

Although the road to a successful treatment seems long, we have promising candidates and strategies that have brought us much further along than we were just five years ago. Investigators are also hopeful that when a successful therapy for prion disease is developed, it will suggest effective therapies for more common neurodegenerative diseases, including Alzheimer's, Parkinson's and amyotrophic lateral sclerosis (ALS). Aberrant, aggregated proteins feature in all these diseases, and so lessons learned from prions may be applicable to them as well.

More to Explore

Prions. Stanley B. Prusiner. 1997 Nobel Prize lecture. Available from the Nobel Foundation site at: **www.nobel.se/medicine/laureates/1997/index.html**

Prion Biology and Diseases. Second edition. Edited by Stanley B. Prusiner. Cold Spring Harbor Laboratory Press, 2004.

Advancing Prion Science: Guidance for the National Prion Research Program. Edited by Rick Erdtmann and Laura B. Sivitz. National Academy Press, 2004.

The Author

STANLEY B. PRUSINER is professor of neurology and biochemistry at the University of California San Francisco School of Medicine. He is a member of the National Academy of Sciences, the Institute of Medicine and the American Philosophical Society. In 1997 he won the Nobel Prize in Physiology or Medicine for his discovery of and research into prions. This is his third article for *Scientific American*. In the spirit of disclosure, Prusiner notes that he founded a company, InPro Biotechnology, which offers several prion tests, some of which are licensed to Beckman Coulter.

5. "Hope in a Vial"

by Carol Ezzell

Will there be an AIDS vaccine anytime soon?

It wasn't supposed to be this hard. When HIV, the virus responsible for AIDS, was first identified in 1984, Margaret M. Heckler, then secretary of the U.S. Department of Health and Human Services, predicted that a vaccine to protect against the scourge would be available within two years. Would that it had been so straightforward.

Roughly 20 years into the pandemic, 40 million people on the planet are infected with HIV, and three million died from it last year (20,000 in North America). Although several potential AIDS vaccines are in clinical tests, so far none has lived up to its early promise. Time and again researchers have obtained tantalizing preliminary results only to run up against a brick wall later. As recently as two years ago, AIDS researchers were saying privately that they doubted whether even a partially protective vaccine would be available in their lifetime.

No stunning breakthroughs have occurred since that time, but a trickle of encouraging data is prompting hope to spring anew in the breasts of even jaded AIDS vaccine hunters. After traveling down blind alleys for more than a decade, they are emerging battered but not beaten, ready to strike out in new directions. "It's an interesting time for AIDS vaccine research," observes Gregg Gonsalves, director of treatment and prevention advocacy for Gay Men's Health Crisis in New York City. "I feel like it's Act Two now."

In the theater, Act One serves to introduce the characters and set the scene; in Act Two, conflict deepens and the real action begins. Act One of AIDS vaccine research debuted HIV, one of the first so-called retroviruses to cause a serious human disease. Unlike most other viruses, retroviruses insinuate their genetic material into that of the body cells they invade, causing the viral genes to become a permanent fixture in the infected cells and in the offspring of those cells. Retroviruses also reproduce rapidly and sloppily, providing ample opportunity for the emergence of mutations that allow HIV to shift its identity and thereby give the immune system or antiretroviral drugs the slip.

Overview/AIDS Vaccines

- Final results from the first large-scale test of a possible AIDS vaccine will be available at the end of this year, but few researchers are optimistic it will work.
- Scientists are now aiming to generate potential AIDS vaccines that stimulate both arms of the immune system: killer cells and antibodies.
- There are five main subtypes, or clades, of HIV. Researchers are debating whether it will be important to devise vaccines for a given area based on the predominant clade infecting that area.

Act One also spotlighted HIV's opposition—the body's immune response—which consists of antibodies (Y-shaped molecules that stick to and tag invaders such as viruses for destruction) and cytotoxic, or killer, T cells (white blood cells charged with destroying virus-infected cells). For years after infection, the immune system battles mightily against HIV, pitting millions of new cytotoxic T cells against the billions of virus particles hatched from infected cells every day. In addition, the immune system deploys armies of antibodies targeted at HIV, at least early in the course of HIV infection, although the antibodies prove relatively ineffectual against this particular foe.

As the curtain rises for Act Two, HIV still has the stage. Results from the first large-scale trial of an AIDS vaccine should become available at the end of this year, but few scientists are optimistic about it: a preliminary analysis suggests that it works poorly. Meanwhile controversy surrounds a giant, U.S.-government-sponsored trial of another potential vaccine slated to begin this September in Thailand. But waiting in the wings are several approaches that are causing the AIDS research community to sit up and take notice. The strategies are reviving the debate about whether, to be useful, a vaccine must elicit immune responses that totally prevent HIV from colonizing a person's cells or whether a vaccine that falls somewhat short of that mark could be acceptable. Some scientists see potential value in vaccines that would elicit the kinds of immune responses that kick in soon after a virus establishes a foothold in cells. By constraining viral replication more effectively than the body's natural responses would, such vaccines, they argue, might at least help prolong the lives of HIV-infected people and delay the onset of the symptomatic, AIDS phase of the disease.

In the early 1990s scientists thought they could figure out the best vaccine strategy for preventing AIDS by studying long-term nonprogressors, people who appeared to have harbored HIV for a decade or more but who hadn't yet fallen ill with AIDS. Sadly, many of the nonprogressors have become ill after all. The key to their relative longevity seems to have been "a weakened virus and/or a strengthened immune system," says John P. Moore of Weill Medical College of Cornell University. In other words, they were lucky enough to have encountered a slow-growing form of HIV at a time when their bodies had the ammunition to keep it at bay.

Not Found in Nature?

AIDS VACCINE developers have struggled for decades to find the "correlates of immunity" for HIV—the magic combination of immune responses that, once induced by a vaccine, would protect someone against infection. But they keep coming up empty-handed, which leaves them with no road map to guide them in the search for an AIDS vaccine. "We're trying to elicit an immune response not found in nature," admits Max Essex of the Harvard School of Public Health. As a result, the quest for an AIDS vaccine has been a bit scattershot.

To be proved useful, a candidate AIDS vaccine must successfully pass through three stages of human testing. In phase I, researchers administer the vaccine to dozens of people to assess its safety and to establish an appropriate dose. Phase II involves hundreds of people and looks more closely at the vaccine's immuno-genicity, its ability to prompt an immune response. In phase III, the potential vaccine is given to thousands of volunteers who are followed for a long time to see whether it protects them from infection. Phase III trials for any drug tend to be costly and difficult to administer. And the AIDS trials are especially challenging because of an ironic requirement: subjects who receive the vaccine must be counseled extensively on how to reduce their chances of infection. They are told, for instance, to use condoms or, in the case of intravenous drug users, clean needles because HIV is spread through sex or blood-to-blood contact. Yet the study will yield results only if some people don't heed the counseling and become exposed anyway.

The first potential vaccine to have reached phase III consists of gp120, a protein that studs the outer envelope of HIV and that the virus uses to latch onto and infect cells. In theory, at least, the presence of gp120 in the bloodstream should activate the recipient's immune system, causing it to quickly mount an attack targeted to gp120 if HIV later finds its way into the body.

World AIDS Snapshot

MOST OF THE GLOBE'S 40 million people infected with HIV live in sub-Saharan Africa and South and Southeast Asia, as reflected in the ranking below, which is based on 2001 data from the Joint United Nations Program on HIV/AIDS. There are five major strains

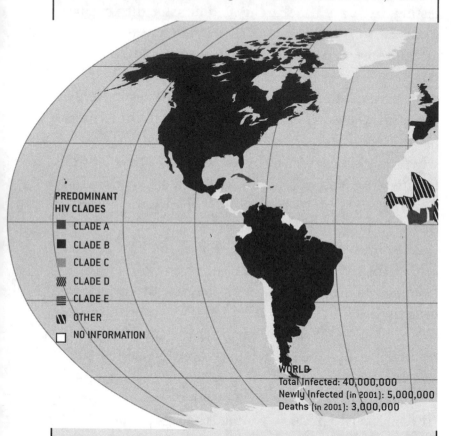

PREDOMINANT HIV CLADES

- CLADE A
- CLADE B
- CLADE C
- CLADE D
- CLADE E
- OTHER
- NO INFORMATION

WORLD
Total Infected: 40,000,000
Newly Infected (in 2001): 5,000,000
Deaths (in 2001): 3,000,000

1 SUB-SAHARAN AFRICA
Total Infected: 28,100,000
Newly Infected: 3,400,000
Deaths: 2,300,000

2 SOUTH/SOUTHEAST ASIA
Total Infected: 6,100,000
Newly Infected: 800,000
Deaths: 400,000

3 LATIN AMERICA
Total Infected: 1,400,000
Newly Infected: 130,000
Deaths: 80,000

4 EAST ASIA/PACIFIC IS.
Total Infected: 1,000,000
Newly Infected: 270,000
Deaths: 35,000

5 E. EUROPE/C. ASIA
Total Infected: 1,000,000
Newly Infected: 250,000
Deaths: 23,000

6 NORTH AMERICA
Total Infected: 940,000
Newly Infected: 45,000
Deaths: 20,000

of HIV, which are also called clades. Although more than one clade can usually be found in any given area, the map highlights the predominant clade affecting each region. The boundaries between prevailing clades are not exact; they change frequently.

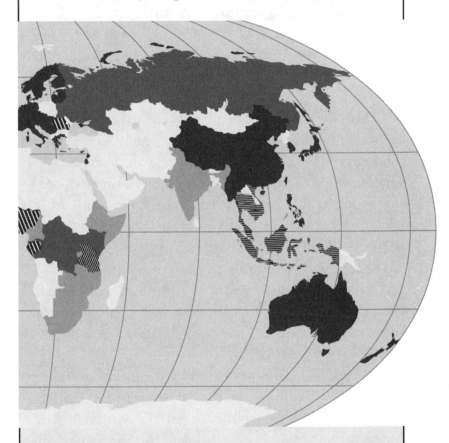

7 WESTERN EUROPE
Total Infected: 560,000
Newly Infected: 30,000
Deaths: 6,800

8 N. AFRICA/MIDDLE EAST
Total Infected: 440,000
Newly Infected: 80,000
Deaths: 30,000

9 CARIBBEAN
Total Infected: 420,000
Newly Infected: 60,000
Deaths: 30,000

10 AUSTRALIA/NEW ZEALAND
Total Infected: 15,000
Newly Infected: 500
Deaths: 120

This vaccine, which is produced by VaxGen in Brisbane, Calif.—a spin-off of biotech juggernaut Genentech in South San Francisco—is being tested in more than 5,400 people (mostly homosexual men) in North America and Europe and in roughly 2,500 intravenous drug users in Southeast Asia. The results from the North American/European trial, which began in 1998, are expected to be announced near the end of this year.

Many AIDS researchers are skeptical of VaxGen's approach because gp120 normally occurs in clumps of three on the surface of the virus, and the company's vaccine employs the molecule in its monomeric, or single-molecule, form. Moreover, vaccines made of just protein generally elicit only an antibody, or humoral, response, without greatly stimulating the cellular arm of the immune system, the part that includes activity by cytotoxic T cells. A growing contingent of investigators suspect that an antibody response alone is not sufficient; a strong cellular response must also be elicited to prevent AIDS.

Indeed, the early findings do not seem encouraging. Last October an independent data-monitoring panel did a preliminary analysis of the results of the North American/European data. Although the panel conducted the analysis primarily to ascertain that the vaccine was causing no dangerous side effects in the volunteers, the reviewers were empowered to recommend halting the trial early if the vaccine appeared to be working. They did not.

For its part, VaxGen asserts that it will seek U.S. Food and Drug Administration approval to sell the vaccine even if the phase III trials show that it reduces a person's likelihood of infection by as little as 30 percent. Company president and co-founder Donald P. Francis points out that the first polio vaccine, developed by Jonas Salk in 1954, was only 60 percent effective, yet it slashed the incidence of polio in the U.S. quickly and dramatically.

This approach could backfire, though, if people who receive a partially effective AIDS vaccine believe they are then protected from infection and can engage in risky behaviors. Karen M. Kuntz and Elizabeth Bogard of the Harvard School of Public Health have constructed a computer model simulating the effects of such a vaccine in a group of injection drug users in Thailand. According to their model, a 30 percent effective vaccine would not slow the spread of AIDS in a community if 90 percent of the people who received it went back to sharing needles or using dirty needles. They found that such reversion to risky behavior would not wash out the public health benefit if a vaccine were at least 75 percent effective.

The controversial study set to begin in Thailand is also a large-scale phase III trial, involving nearly 16,000 people. It combines the VaxGen vaccine with a canarypox virus into which scientists have stitched genes that encode gp120 as well as two other proteins—one that makes up the HIV core and one that allows it to reproduce. Because this genetically engineered canarypox virus (made by Aventis Pasteur, headquartered

One AIDS Vaccine Strategy

A VACCINE APPROACH being pioneered by Merck involves an initial injection of a naked DNA vaccine followed months later by a booster shot of crippled, genetically altered adenovirus particles. Both are designed to elicit an immune response targeted to the HIV core protein, Gag, and to primarily arouse the cellular arm of the immune system—the one that uses cytotoxic T cells to destroy virus-infected cells. The naked DNA vaccine also results in the production of antibody molecules against Gag, but such antibodies are not very useful in fighting HIV.

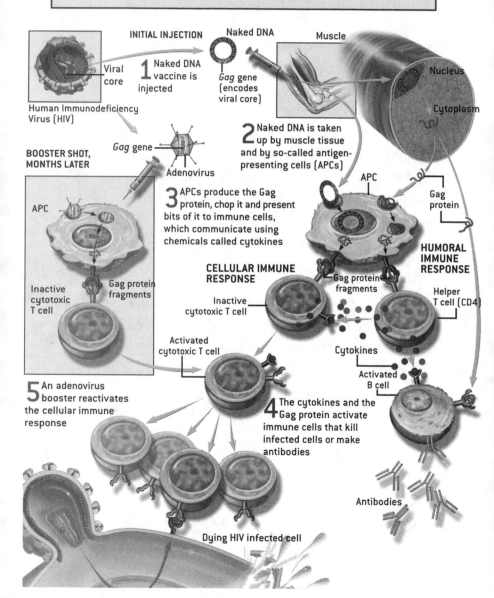

INITIAL INJECTION Naked DNA Muscle

Viral core

1 Naked DNA vaccine is injected

Gag gene (encodes viral core)

Nucleus

Cytoplasm

Human Immunodeficiency Virus (HIV)

2 Naked DNA is taken up by muscle tissue and by so-called antigen-presenting cells (APCs)

BOOSTER SHOT, MONTHS LATER

Gag gene

Adenovirus

APC

Gag protein

3 APCs produce the Gag protein, chop it and present bits of it to immune cells, which communicate using chemicals called cytokines

APC

Inactive cytotoxic T cell

Gag protein fragments

CELLULAR IMMUNE RESPONSE

Inactive cytotoxic T cell

Gag protein fragments

HUMORAL IMMUNE RESPONSE

Helper T cell (CD4)

Activated cytotoxic T cell

Cytokines

Activated B cell

5 An adenovirus booster reactivates the cellular immune response

4 The cytokines and the Gag protein activate immune cells that kill infected cells or make antibodies

Antibodies

Dying HIV infected cell

in Lyons, France) enters cells and causes them to display fragments of HIV on their surface, it stimulates the cellular arm of the immune system.

Political wrangling and questions over its scientific value have slowed widespread testing of the gp120/canarypox vaccine. Initially the National Institute of Allergy and Infectious Diseases (NIAID) and the U.S. Department of Defense were scheduled to conduct essentially duplicate trials of the vaccine. But NIAID pulled the plug on its trial after an examination of the data from a phase II study showed that fewer than 30 percent of the volunteers generated cytotoxic T cells against HIV. And in a bureaucratic twist, this past January the White House transferred the budget for the Defense Department trial over to NIAID as part of an effort to streamline AIDS research.

Peggy Johnston, assistant director of AIDS vaccines for NIAID, says she expects there will be a trial of the vaccine but emphasizes that "it will be a Thai trial; we won't have any [NIAID] people there on the ground running things."

Critics cite these machinations as a case study of politics getting in the way of progress against AIDS. "There's little science involved" in the trial, claims one skeptic, who wonders why the Thais aren't asking, "'If it's not good enough for America, how come it's good enough for us?'" Others point out that the trial, which was conceived by the Defense Department, will answer only the question of whether the vaccine works; it won't collect any data that scientists could use to explain its potential failure.

Partial Protection

INTO THIS SCENE comes Merck, which is completing separate phase I trials of two different vaccine candidates that it has begun to test together. In February, Emilio A. Emini, Merck's senior vice president for vaccine research, wowed scientists attending the Ninth Conference on Retroviruses and Opportunistic Infections in Seattle with the company's initial data from the two trials.

The first trial is investigating a potential vaccine composed of only the HIV *gag* gene, which encodes the virus's core protein. It is administered as a so-called naked DNA vaccine, consisting solely of DNA. Cells take up the gene and use it as a blueprint for making the viral protein, which in turn stimulates a mild (and probably unhelpful) humoral response and a more robust cellular response [*see illustration on page 90*]. Emini and his colleagues reported that 42 percent of volunteers who received the highest dose of the naked DNA vaccine raised cytotoxic T cells capable of attacking HIV-infected cells.

The second trial employs the HIV *gag* gene spliced into a crippled adenovirus, the class responsible for many common colds. This altered adenovirus ferries the *gag* gene into cells, which then make the HIV core protein and elicit an immune response targeted to that protein. Emini told the conference that between 44 and 67 percent of people who received injections of the adenovirus-based vaccine generated a cellular immune response that varied in intensity according to the size of the dose the subjects received and how long ago they got their shots.

Merck is now beginning to test a combination of the DNA and adenovirus approaches because Emini predicts that the vaccines will work best when administered as part of the same regimen. "The concept," he says, "is not that the DNA vaccine will be a good vaccine on its own, but that it may work as a primer of the immune system," to be followed months later by a booster shot of the adenovirus vaccine. A possible stumbling block is that most people have had colds caused by adenoviruses. Accordingly, the immune systems of such individuals would already have an arsenal in place that could wipe out the adenovirus vaccine before it had a chance to deliver its payload of HIV genes and stimulate AIDS immunity. Increasing the dose of the adenovirus vaccine could get around this obstacle.

Emini says he and his co-workers are emphasizing cellular immunity in part because of the disappointing results so far with vaccines designed to engender humoral responses. "Antibodies continue to be a problem," he admits. "There are a handful of reasonably potent antibodies isolated from HIV-infected people, but we haven't figured out how to raise those antibodies using a vaccine."

Lawrence Corey of the Fred Hutchinson Cancer Research Center in Seattle agrees: "You'd like to have both [a cellular and an antibody response], but the greatest progress has been in eliciting a cellular response," says Corey, who is also principal investigator of the federally funded HIV Vaccine Trials Network.

Antibodies are important, too, because they are the immune system's first line of defense and are thought to be the key to preventing viruses from ever contacting the cells they infect. Corey says that vaccines that are designed primarily to evoke cellular immunity (as are Merck's) are not likely to prevent infection but should give someone a head start in combating the virus if he or she does become infected. "Instead of progressing to AIDS in eight years, you progress in 25 years," he predicts. But, Corey adds, it is unclear whether a vaccine that only slowed disease progression would stem the AIDS pandemic, because people would still be able to spread the infection to others despite having less virus in their bloodstream.

Finding a way to induce the production of antibodies able to neutralize HIV has been hard slogging for several reasons. For one, the virus's shape-shifting ways allow it to stay one step ahead of the immune response. "The thing that distinguishes HIV from all other human viruses is its ability to mutate so fast," Essex says. "By the time you make a neutralizing antibody [against HIV], it is only against the virus that was in you a month ago."

According to many scientists, vaccines using a logical molecule, gp120—the protein the virus uses to invade immune cells, as discussed above—haven't worked, probably because the antibodies that such vaccines elicit bind to the wrong part of the molecule. Gp120 shields the precise binding site it uses to latch onto CD4, its docking site on immune cells, until the last nanosecond, when it snaps open like a jackknife. One way to get around this problem, suggested in a paper published in *Science* three years ago by Jack H. Nunberg of the University of Montana and his colleagues, would be to make vaccines of gp120 molecules that have previously been exposed to CD4 and therefore have already sprung open. But those results have been "difficult to replicate," according to Corey, making researchers pessimistic about the approach.

Another possible hurdle to getting an AIDS vaccine that elicits effective anti-HIV antibodies is the variety of HIV subtypes, or clades, that affect different areas of the world. There are five major clades, designated A through E [*see illustration on pages 86–87*]. Although clade B is the predominant strain in North America and Europe, most of sub-Saharan Africa—the hardest-hit region of the globe—has clade C. The ones primarily responsible for AIDS in South and Southeast Asia—the second biggest AIDS hot spot—are clades B, C and E.

Several studies indicate that antibodies that recognize AIDS viruses from one clade might not bind to viruses from other clades, suggesting that a vaccine made from the strain found in the U.S. might not protect people in South Africa, for example. But scientists disagree about the significance of clade differences and whether only strains that match the most prevalent clade in a given area can be tested in countries there. Essex, who is gearing up to lead phase I tests of a clade C–based vaccine in Botswana later this year, argues that unless researchers are sure that a vaccine designed against one clade can cross-react with viruses from another, they must stick to testing vaccines that use the clade prevalent in the populations being studied. Cross-reactivity could occur under ideal circumstances, but, he says, "unless we know that, it's important for us to use subtype-specific vaccines."

Using the corresponding clade also avoids the appearance that people in developing countries are being used as guinea pigs for testing a vaccine that is designed to work only in the U.S. or Europe. VaxGen's tests in Thailand are based on a combination of clades B and E, and in April the International AIDS Vaccine Initiative expanded tests of a clade A–derived vaccine in Kenya, where clade A is found.

But in January, Malegapuru William Makgoba and Nandipha Solomon of the Medical Research Council of South Africa, together with Timothy Johan Paul Tucker of the South African AIDS Vaccine Initiative, wrote in the *British Medical Journal* that the relevance of HIV subtypes "remains unresolved." They assert that clades "have assumed a political and national importance, which could interfere with important international trials of efficacy."

Early data from the Merck vaccine trials suggest that clade differences blur when it comes to cellular immunity. At the retrovirus conference in February,

Emini reported that killer cells from 10 of 13 people who received a vaccine based on clade B also reacted in laboratory tests to viral proteins from clade A or C viruses. "There is a potential for a substantial cross-clade response" in cellular immunity, he says, "but that's not going to hold true for antibodies." Corey concurs that clade variation "is likely to play much, much less of a role" for killer cells than for antibodies because most cytotoxic T cells recognize parts of HIV that are the same from clade to clade.

Johnston of NIAID theorizes that one answer would be to use all five major clades in every vaccine. Chiron in Emeryville, Calif., is developing a multiclade vaccine, which is in early clinical trials. Such an approach could be overkill, however, Johnston says. It could be that proteins from only one clade would be recognized "and the other proteins would be wasted," she warns.

Whatever the outcome on the clade question, Moore of Weill Medical College says he and fellow researchers are more hopeful than they were a few years ago about their eventual ability to devise an AIDS vaccine that would elicit both killer cells and antibodies. "The problem is not impossible," he says, "just extremely difficult."

More to Explore

HIV Vaccine Efforts Inch Forward. Brian Vastag in *Journal of the American Medical Association*, Vol. 286, No. 15, pages 1826–1828; October 17, 2001.

For an overview of AIDS vaccine research, including
the status of U.S.-funded AIDS clinical trials,
visit **www.niaid.nih.gov/daids/vaccine/default.htm**
A global perspective on the AIDS pandemic and the
need for a vaccine can be found at the International
AIDS Vaccine Initiative Web site: **www.iavi.org**
Joint United Nations Program on HIV/AIDS:
www.unaids.org

The Author

CAROL EZZELL is a staff editor and writer.

6. "Edible Vaccines"

by William H. R. Langridge

*One day children may get immunized by munching on foods
instead of enduring shots. More important, food vaccines might
save millions who now die for lack of access to traditional inoculants*

Vaccines have accomplished near miracles in the
fight against infectious disease. They have consigned
smallpox to history and should soon do the same for
polio. By the late 1990s an international campaign to
immunize all the world's children against six devastating
diseases was reportedly reaching 80 percent of infants
(up from about 5 percent in the mid-1970s) and was
reducing the annual death toll from those infections by
roughly three million.

Yet these victories mask tragic gaps in delivery. The
20 percent of infants still missed by the six vaccines—
against diphtheria, pertussis (whooping cough), polio,
measles, tetanus and tuberculosis—account for about
two million unnecessary deaths each year, especially in
the most remote and impoverished parts of the globe.
Upheavals in many developing nations now threaten to
erode the advances of the recent past, and millions still
die from infectious diseases for which immunizations
are nonexistent, unreliable or too costly.

This situation is worrisome not only for the places
that lack health care but for the entire world. Regions
harboring infections that have faded from other areas

are like bombs ready to explode. When environmental or social disasters undermine sanitation systems or displace communities—bringing people with little immunity into contact with carriers—infections that have been long gone from a population can come roaring back. Further, as international travel and trade make the earth a smaller place, diseases that arise in one locale are increasingly popping up continents away. Until everyone has routine access to vaccines, no one will be entirely safe.

In the early 1990s Charles J. Arntzen, then at Texas A&M University, conceived of a way to solve many of the problems that bar vaccines from reaching all too many children in developing nations. Soon after learning of a World Health Organization call for inexpensive, oral vaccines that needed no refrigeration, Arntzen visited Bangkok, where he saw a mother soothe a crying baby by offering a piece of banana. Plant biologists had already devised ways of introducing selected genes (the blueprints for proteins) into plants and inducing the altered, or "transgenic," plants to manufacture the encoded proteins. Perhaps, he mused, food could be genetically engineered to produce vaccines in their edible parts, which could then be eaten when inoculations were needed.

The advantages would be enormous. The plants could be grown locally, and cheaply, using the standard growing methods of a given region. Because many food plants can be regenerated readily, the crops could potentially be produced indefinitely without the growers having to purchase more seeds or plants year after year. Homegrown vaccines would also avoid the logistical and economic problems posed by having to transport traditional preparations over long distances, keeping them cold en route and at their destination. And, being edible, the vaccines would require no syringes—which, aside from costing something, can lead to infections if they become contaminated.

Efforts to make Arntzen's inspired vision a reality are still quite preliminary. Yet studies carried out in animals over the past 10 years, and small tests in people, encourage hope that edible vaccines can work. The research has also fueled speculation that certain food vaccines might help suppress autoimmunity—in which the body's defenses mistakenly attack normal, uninfected tissues. Among the autoimmune disorders that might be prevented or eased are type I diabetes (the kind that commonly arises during childhood), multiple sclerosis and rheumatoid arthritis.

By Any Other Name . . .

Regardless of how vaccines for infectious diseases are delivered, they all have the same aim: priming the immune system to swiftly destroy specific disease-causing agents, or pathogens, before the agents can multiply enough to cause symptoms. Classically, this priming has been achieved by presenting the immune system with whole viruses or bacteria that have been killed or made too weak to proliferate much.

On detecting the presence of a foreign organism in a vaccine, the immune system behaves as if the body were under attack by a fully potent antagonist. It mobilizes its various forces to root out and destroy the apparent invader—targeting the campaign to specific antigens (proteins recognized as foreign). The acute response soon abates, but it leaves behind sentries, known as "memory" cells, that remain on alert, ready to unleash whole armies of defenders if the real pathogen ever finds its way into the body. Some vaccines provide lifelong protection; others (such as those for cholera and tetanus) must be readministered periodically.

Classic vaccines pose a small but troubling risk that the vaccine microorganisms will somehow spring back to life, causing the diseases they were meant to forestall. For that reason, vaccine makers today favor so-called subunit preparations, composed primarily of antigenic proteins divorced from a pathogen's genes. On their own, the proteins have no way of establishing an infection. Subunit vaccines, however, are expensive, in part because they are produced in cultures of bacteria or animal cells and have to be purified out; they also need to be refrigerated.

Food vaccines are like subunit preparations in that they are engineered to contain antigens but bear no genes that would enable whole pathogens to form. Ten years ago Arntzen understood that edible vaccines would therefore be as safe as subunit preparations while sidestepping their costs and demands for purification and refrigeration. But before he and others could study the effects of food vaccines in people, they had to obtain positive answers to a number of questions. Would plants engineered to carry antigen genes produce functional copies of the specified proteins? When the food plants were fed to test animals, would the antigens be degraded in the stomach before having a chance to act? (Typical subunit vaccines have to be delivered by injection precisely because of such degradation.) If the antigens did survive, would they, in fact, attract the immune system's attention? And would the response be strong enough to defend the animals against infection?

Additionally, researchers wanted to know whether edible vaccines would elicit what is known as mucosal immunity. Many pathogens enter the body through the nose, mouth or other openings. Hence, the first defenses they encounter are those in the mucous membranes that line the airways, the digestive tract and the reproductive tract; these membranes constitute the biggest pathogen-deterring surface in the body. When the mucosal immune response is effective, it generates molecules known as secretory antibodies that dash into the cavities of those passageways, neutralizing any pathogens they find. An effective reaction also activates a systemic response, in which circulating cells of the immune system help to destroy invaders at distant sites.

Injected vaccines initially bypass mucous membranes and typically do a poor job of stimulating mucosal immune responses. But edible vaccines come into contact with the lining of the digestive tract. In theory, then, they would activate both mucosal and systemic

How to Make an Edible Vaccine

One way of generating edible vaccines relies on the bacterium *Agrobacterium tumefaciens* to deliver into plant cells the genetic blueprints for viral or bacterial "antigens"—proteins that elicit a targeted immune response in the recipient. The diagram illustrates the production of vaccine potatoes.

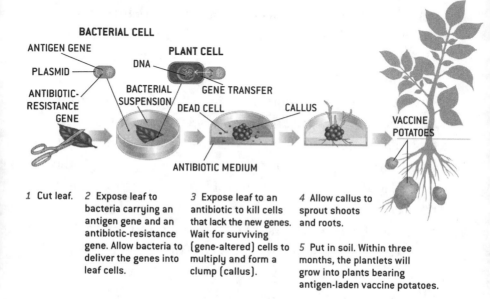

BACTERIAL CELL

ANTIGEN GENE

PLASMID

ANTIBIOTIC-RESISTANCE GENE

PLANT CELL

DNA

BACTERIAL SUSPENSION

GENE TRANSFER

DEAD CELL

CALLUS

VACCINE POTATOES

ANTIBIOTIC MEDIUM

1 Cut leaf.

2 Expose leaf to bacteria carrying an antigen gene and an antibiotic-resistance gene. Allow bacteria to deliver the genes into leaf cells.

3 Expose leaf to an antibiotic to kill cells that lack the new genes. Wait for surviving (gene-altered) cells to multiply and form a clump (callus).

4 Allow callus to sprout shoots and roots.

5 Put in soil. Within three months, the plantlets will grow into plants bearing antigen-laden vaccine potatoes.

immunity. That dual effect should, in turn, help improve protection against many dangerous microorganisms, including, importantly, the kinds that cause diarrhea.

Those of us attempting to develop food vaccines place a high priority on combating diarrhea. Together the main causes—the Norwalk virus, rotavirus, *Vibrio cholerae* (the cause of cholera) and enterotoxigenic *Escherichia coli* (a toxin-producing source of "traveler's diarrhea")—account for some three million infant deaths a year, mainly in developing nations. These pathogens disrupt cells of the small intestine in ways that cause water to flow from the blood and tissues into the intestine. The resulting dehydration may be combated by delivering an intravenous or oral solution of electrolytes, but it often turns deadly when rehydration therapy is not an option. No vaccine practical for wide distribution in the developing nations is yet available to prevent these ills.

By 1995 researchers attempting to answer the many questions before them had established that plants could indeed manufacture foreign antigens in their proper conformations. For instance, Arntzen and his colleagues had introduced into tobacco plants the gene for a protein derived from the hepatitis B virus and had gotten the plants to synthesize the protein. When they injected the antigen into mice, it activated the same immune system components that are activated by the virus itself. (Hepatitis B can damage the liver and contribute to liver cancer.)

Green Lights on Many Fronts

But injection is not the aim; feeding is. In the past five years experiments conducted by Arntzen (who moved to the Boyce Thompson Institute for Plant Research at Cornell University in 1995) and his collaborators and by my group at Loma Linda University have demonstrated that tomato or potato plants can synthesize

antigens from the Norwalk virus, enterotoxigenic
E. coli, *V. cholerae* and the hepatitis B virus. Moreover,
feeding antigen-laced tubers or fruits to test animals
can evoke mucosal and systemic immune responses
that fully or partly protect animals from subsequent
exposure to the real pathogens or, in the case of
V. cholerae and enterotoxigenic *E. coli*, to microbial
toxins. Edible vaccines have also provided laboratory
animals with some protection against challenge by the
rabies virus, *Helicobacter pylori* (a bacterial cause of
ulcers) and the mink enteric virus (which does not
affect humans).

It is not entirely surprising that antigens delivered
in plant foods survive the trip through the stomach
well enough to reach and activate the immune system.
The tough outer wall of plant cells apparently serves
as temporary armor for the antigens, keeping them
relatively safe from gastric secretions. When the wall
finally begins to break up in the intestines, the cells
gradually release their antigenic cargo.

Of course, the key question is whether food vaccines
can be useful in people. The era of clinical trials for
this technology is just beginning. Nevertheless, Arntzen
and his collaborators obtained reassuring results in the
first published human trial, involving about a dozen
subjects. In 1997 volunteers who ate pieces of peeled,
raw potatoes containing a benign segment of the *E. coli*
toxin (the part called the B subunit) displayed both
mucosal and systemic immune responses. Since then,
the group has also seen immune reactivity in 19 of 20

people who ate a potato vaccine aimed at the Norwalk virus. Similarly, after Hilary Koprowski of Thomas Jefferson University fed transgenic lettuce carrying a hepatitis B antigen to three volunteers, two of the subjects displayed a good systemic response. Whether edible vaccines can actually protect against human disease remains to be determined, however.

Still to Be Accomplished

In short, the studies completed so far in animals and people have provided a proof of principle; they indicate that the strategy is feasible. Yet many issues must still be addressed. For one, the amount of vaccine made by a plant is low. Production can be increased in different ways—for instance, by linking antigen genes with regulatory elements known to help switch on the genes more readily. As researchers solve that challenge, they will also have to ensure that any given amount of a vaccine food provides a predictable dose of antigen.

Additionally, workers could try to enhance the odds that antigens will activate the immune system instead of passing out of the body unused. General stimulators (adjuvants) and better targeting to the immune system might compensate in part for low antigen production.

One targeting strategy involves linking antigens to molecules that bind well to immune system components known as M cells in the intestinal lining. M cells take in samples of materials that have entered the small intestine (including pathogens) and pass them to other cells of the immune system, such as antigen-presenting cells. Macrophages and other antigen-presenting cells chop up their acquisitions and display the resulting protein fragments on the cell surface. If white blood cells called helper T lymphocytes recognize the fragments as foreign, they may induce B lymphocytes (B cells) to secrete neutralizing antibodies and may also help initiate a broader attack on the perceived enemy.

It turns out that an innocuous segment of the *V. cholerae* toxin—the B subunit—binds readily to a molecule on M cells that ushers foreign material into those cells. By fusing antigens from other pathogens to this subunit, it should be possible to improve the uptake of antigens by M cells and to enhance immune responses to the added antigens. The B subunit also tends to associate with copies of itself, forming a doughnut-shaped, five-membered ring with a hole in the middle. These features raise the prospect of producing a vaccine that brings several different antigens to M cells at once—thus potentially fulfilling an urgent need for a single vaccine that can protect against multiple diseases simultaneously.

Researchers are also grappling with the reality that plants sometimes grow poorly when they start producing large amounts of a foreign protein. One solution would be to equip plants with regulatory elements that cause antigen genes to turn on—that is, give rise to the encoded antigens—only at selected times (such as after a plant is nearly fully grown or is exposed to some outside activator molecule) or only in its edible regions. This work is progressing.

Further, each type of plant poses its own challenges. Potatoes are ideal in many ways because they can be propagated from "eyes" and can be stored for long periods without refrigeration. But potatoes usually have to be cooked to be palatable, and heating can denature proteins. Indeed, as is true of tobacco plants, potatoes were not initially intended to be used as vaccine vehicles; they were studied because they were easy to manipulate. Surprisingly, though, some kinds of potatoes are actually eaten raw in South America. Also, contrary to expectations, cooking of potatoes does not always destroy the full complement of antigen. So potatoes may have more practical merit than most of us expected.

Bananas need no cooking and are grown widely in developing nations, but banana trees take a few years to mature, and the fruit spoils fairly rapidly after ripening. Tomatoes grow more quickly and are cultivated broadly, but they too may rot readily. Inexpensive methods of preserving these foods—such as drying— might overcome the spoilage problem. Among the other foods under consideration are lettuce, carrots, peanuts, rice, wheat, corn and soybeans.

In another concern, scientists need to be sure that vaccines meant to enhance immune responses do not backfire and suppress immunity instead. Research into a phenomenon called oral tolerance has shown that ingesting certain proteins can at times cause the body to

How Edible Vaccines Provide Protection

An antigen in a food vaccine gets taken up by M cells in the intestine (*below, left*) and passed to various immune-system cells, which then launch a defensive attack—as if the antigen were a true infectious agent, not just part of one. That response leaves long-lasting "memory" cells able to promptly neutralize the real infectious agent if it attempts an invasion (*right*).

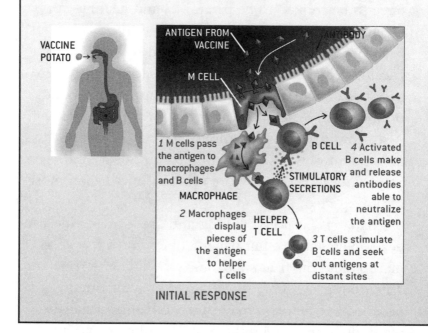

VACCINE POTATO

ANTIGEN FROM VACCINE

ANTIBODY

M CELL

1 M cells pass the antigen to macrophages and B cells

MACROPHAGE

2 Macrophages display pieces of the antigen to helper T cells

HELPER T CELL

STIMULATORY SECRETIONS

B CELL

3 T cells stimulate B cells and seek out antigens at distant sites

4 Activated B cells make and release antibodies able to neutralize the antigen

INITIAL RESPONSE

shut down its responses to those proteins. To determine safe, effective doses and feeding schedules for edible vaccines, manufacturers will need to gain a better handle on the manipulations that influence whether an orally delivered antigen will stimulate or depress immunity.

A final issue worth studying is whether food vaccines ingested by mothers can indirectly vaccinate their

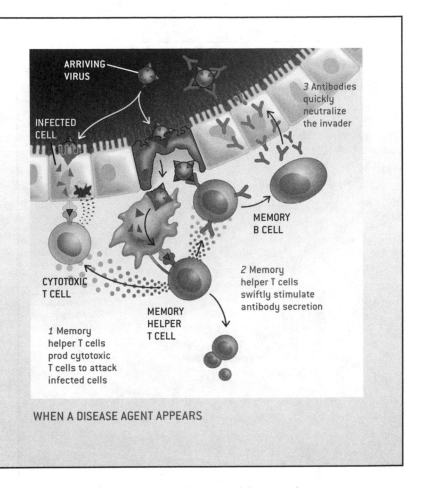

ARRIVING VIRUS

INFECTED CELL

3 Antibodies quickly neutralize the invader

MEMORY B CELL

CYTOTOXIC T CELL

2 Memory helper T cells swiftly stimulate antibody secretion

MEMORY HELPER T CELL

1 Memory helper T cells prod cytotoxic T cells to attack infected cells

WHEN A DISEASE AGENT APPEARS

babies. In theory, a mother could eat a banana or two and thus trigger production of antibodies that would travel to her fetus via the placenta or to her infant via breast milk.

Nonscientific challenges accompany the technical ones. Not many pharmaceutical manufacturers are eager to support research for products targeted primarily to markets outside the lucrative West. International aid

Moving Against Malnutrition

As research into edible vaccines is progressing, so too are efforts to make foods more nutritious. A much publicized example, "golden rice," takes aim at vitamin A deficiency, rampant in many parts of Asia, Africa and Latin America. This condition can lead to blindness and to immune impairment, which contributes to the death of more than a million children each year.

Rice would be a convenient way to deliver the needed vitamin, because the grain is a daily staple for a third or more of all people on the earth. But natural varieties do not supply vitamin A. Golden rice, though, has been genetically altered to make beta-carotene, a pigment the body converts to vitamin A.

A team led by Ingo Potrykus of the Swiss Federal Institute of Technology and Peter Beyer of the University of Freiburg in Germany formally reported its creation this past January in *Science*. In May an agribusiness—Zeneca—bought the rights and agreed to allow the rice to be donated to facilities that will cross the beta-carotene trait into rice species popular in impoverished areas and will distribute the resulting products to farmers at no charge. (Zeneca is hoping to make its money from sales of the improved rice in richer countries, where beta-carotene's antioxidant properties are likely to have appeal.)

Golden rice is not yet ready to be commercialized, however. Much testing still lies ahead, including analyses of whether the human body can efficiently absorb the beta-carotene in the rice. Testing is expected to last at least until 2003.

Meanwhile scientists are trying to enrich rice with still more beta-carotene, with other vitamins and with minerals. At a conference last year Potrykus announced success with iron; more than two billion people worldwide are iron deficient.

Investigators are attempting to enhance other foods as well. In June, for instance, a group of British and Japanese investigators reported the creation of a tomato containing a gene able to supply three times the usual amount of beta-carotene. Conventional breeding methods are being used, too, such as in an international project focused on increasing the vitamin and mineral content of rice and four other staples—wheat, corn, beans and cassava.

Not everyone is thrilled by the recent genetic coups. Genetically modified (GM) foods in general remain controversial. Some opponents contend that malnutrition can be combated right now in other ways—say, by constructing supply roads. And they fear that companies will tout the benefits of the new foods to deflect attention from worries over other GM crops, most of which (such as plants designed to resist damage from pesticides) offer fewer clear advantages for consumers. High on the list of concerns are risk to the environment and to people. Supporters of the nutritionally improved foods hope, however, that the rice won't be thrown out with the rinse water.   —*Ricki Rusting, staff writer* organizations and some national governments and philanthropies are striving to fill the gap, but the effort to develop edible vaccines remains underfunded.

In addition, edible vaccines fall under the increasingly unpopular rubric of "genetically modified" plants. Recently a British company (Axis Genetics) that was supporting studies of edible vaccines failed; one of its leaders lays at least part of the blame on investor worry about companies involved with genetically engineered foods. I hope, however, that these vaccines will avoid serious controversy, because they are intended to save lives and would probably be planted over much less acreage than other food plants (if they are raised outside of greenhouses at all). Also, as drugs, they would be subjected to closer scrutiny by regulatory bodies.

Fighting Autoimmunity

Consideration of one of the challenges detailed here—the risk of inducing oral tolerance—has recently led my group and others to pursue edible vaccines as tools for quashing autoimmunity. Although oral delivery of antigens derived from infectious agents often stimulates the immune system, oral delivery of "autoantigens" (proteins derived from uninfected tissue in a treated individual) can sometimes suppress immune activity—a phenomenon seen frequently in test animals. No one fully understands the reasons for this difference.

Some of the evidence that ingesting autoantigens, or "self-antigens," might suppress autoimmunity comes from studies of type I diabetes, which results from autoimmune destruction of the insulin-producing cells

Stopping Autoimmunity

The autoimmune reaction responsible for type I diabetes arises when the immune system mistakes proteins that are made by pancreatic beta cells (the insulin producers) for foreign invaders. The resulting attack, targeted to the offending proteins, or "autoantigens," destroys the beta cells (below, left). Eating small amounts of autoantigens quiets the process in diabetic mice, for unclear reasons. The autoantigens might act in part by switching on "suppressor" cells of the immune system (inset), which then block the destructive activities of their cousins (below, right).

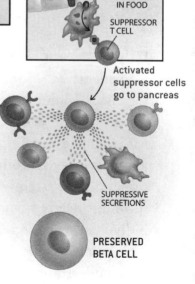

INTESTINAL CAVITY

M CELL

AUTO-ANTIGEN DELIVERED IN FOOD

SUPPRESSOR T CELL

Activated suppressor cells go to pancreas

STIMULATORY SECRETIONS

HELPER T CELL

CYTOTOXIC T CELL

AUTOANTIGEN

NATURAL KILLER CELL

B CELL

DAMAGED AREA

ANTIBODY

BETA CELL UNDER ATTACK IN PANCREAS

DESTRUCTIVE SECRETIONS

MACROPHAGE

BEFORE TREATMENT

SUPPRESSIVE SECRETIONS

PRESERVED BETA CELL

AFTER TREATMENT

(beta cells) of the pancreas. This destruction progresses silently for a time. Eventually, though, the loss of beta cells leads to a drastic shortage of insulin, a hormone needed to help cells take up sugar from the blood for energy. The loss results in high blood sugar levels. Insulin injections help to control diabetes, but they are by no means a cure; diabetics face an elevated risk of severe complications.

In the past 15 years, investigators have identified several beta cell proteins that can elicit autoimmunity in people predisposed to type I diabetes. The main culprits, however, are insulin and a protein called GAD (glutamic acid decarboxylase). Researchers have also made progress in detecting when diabetes is "brewing." The next step, then, is to find ways of stopping the underground process before any symptoms arise.

To that end, my colleagues and I, as well as other groups, have developed plant-based diabetes vaccines, such as potatoes containing insulin or GAD linked to the innocuous B subunit of the *V. cholerae* toxin (to enhance uptake of the antigens by M cells). Feeding of the vaccines to a mouse strain that becomes diabetic helped to suppress the immune attack and to prevent or delay the onset of high blood sugar.

Transgenic plants cannot yet produce the amounts of self-antigens that would be needed for a viable vaccine against human diabetes or other autoimmune diseases. But, as is true for infectious diseases, investigators are exploring a number of promising schemes to overcome that and other challenges.

Edible vaccines for combating autoimmunity and infectious diseases have a long way to go before they will be ready for large-scale testing in people. The technical obstacles, though, all seem surmountable. Nothing would be more satisfying than to protect the health of many millions of now defenseless children around the globe.

More to Explore

Oral Immunization with a Recombinant Bacterial Antigen Produced in Transgenic Plants. Charles J. Arntzen in *Science*, Vol. 268, No. 5211, pages 714–716; May 5, 1995.

Immunogenicity in Humans of a Recombinant Bacterial Antigen Delivered in a Transgenic Potato. C. O. Tacket et al. in *Nature Medicine*, Vol. 4, No. 5, pages 607–609; May 1998.

A Plant-Based Cholera Toxin B Subunit-Insulin Fusion Protein Protects against the Development of Autoimmune Diabetes. Takeshi Arakawa, Jie Yu, D. K. Chong, John Hough, Paul C. Engen and William H. R. Langridge in *Nature Biotechnology*, Vol. 16, No. 10, pages 934–938; October 1998.

Plant-Based Vaccines for Protection against Infectious and Autoimmune Diseases. James E. Carter and William H. R. Langridge in *Critical Reviews in Plant Sciences* (in press).

The Author

WILLIAM H. R. LANGRIDGE, a leader in the
effort to develop edible vaccines for infectious and
autoimmune diseases, is professor in the department of
biochemistry and at the Center for Molecular Biology
and Gene Therapy at the Loma Linda University School
of Medicine. After receiving his Ph.D. in biochemistry
from the University of Massachusetts at Amherst in
1973, he conducted genetic research on insect viruses
and plants at the Boyce Thompson Institute for
Plant Research at Cornell University. In 1987 he
moved to the Plant Biotechnology Center of the
University of Alberta in Edmonton, and he joined
Loma Linda in 1993.

"Beyond
7. Chicken Soup"

by William A. Haseltine

The antiviral era is upon us, with an array of virus-fighting drugs on the market and in development. Research into viral genomes is fueling much of this progress

Back in the mid-1980s, when scientists first learned that a virus caused a relentless new disease named AIDS, pharmacy shelves were loaded with drugs able to treat bacterial infections. For viral diseases, though, medicine had little to offer beyond chicken soup and a cluster of vaccines. The story is dramatically different today. Dozens of antiviral therapies, including several new vaccines, are available, and hundreds more are in development. If the 1950s were the golden age of antibiotics, we are now in the early years of the golden age of antivirals.

This richness springs from various sources. Pharmaceutical companies would certainly point to the advent in the past 15 years of sophisticated techniques for discovering all manner of drugs. At the same time, frantic efforts to find lifesaving therapies for HIV, the cause of AIDS, have suggested creative ways to fight not only HIV but other viruses, too.

A little-recognized but more important force has also been at work: viral genomics, which deciphers the sequence of "letters," or nucleic acids, in a virus's genetic "text." This sequence includes the letters in all the virus's genes, which form the blueprints for viral proteins; these proteins, in turn, serve as the structural elements and the working parts of the virus and thus control its behavior. With a full or even a partial genome sequence in hand, scientists can quickly learn many details of how a virus causes disease—and which stages of the process might be particularly vulnerable to attack. In 2001 the full genome of any virus can be sequenced within days, making it possible to spot that virus's weaknesses with unprecedented speed.

The majority of antivirals on sale these days take aim at HIV, herpesviruses (responsible for a range of ills, from cold sores to encephalitis), and hepatitis B and C viruses (both of which can cause liver cancer). HIV and these forms of hepatitis will surely remain a main focus of investigation for some time; together they cause more than 250,000 cases of disease in the U.S. every year and millions in other countries. Biologists, however, are working aggressively to combat other viral illnesses as well. I cannot begin to describe all the classes of antivirals on the market and under study, but I do hope this article will offer a sense of the extraordinary advances that genomics and other sophisticated technologies have made possible in recent years.

Drug-Search Strategies

THE EARLIEST ANTIVIRALS (mainly against herpes) were introduced in the 1960s and emerged from traditional drug-discovery methods. Viruses are structurally simple,

essentially consisting of genes and perhaps some enzymes
(biological catalysts) encased in a protein capsule and
sometimes also in a lipid envelope. Because this design
requires viruses to replicate inside cells, investigators
infected cells, grew them in culture and exposed the
cultures to chemicals that might plausibly inhibit viral
activities known at the time. Chemicals that reduced
the amount of virus in the culture were considered for
in-depth investigation. Beyond being a rather hit-or-
miss process, such screening left scientists with few
clues to other viral activities worth attacking. This
handicap hampered efforts to develop drugs that were
more effective or had fewer side effects.

Genomics has been a springboard for discovering
fresh targets for attack and has thus opened the way to
development of whole new classes of antiviral drugs.
Most viral targets selected since the 1980s have been
identified with the help of genomics, even though the
term itself was only coined in the late 1980s, well after

Overview/Antiviral Drugs

- Deciphering the genetic sequences, or genomes, of humans and of a variety of
viruses has enabled scientists to devise drugs for diseases such AIDS, hepatitis
and influenza.
- After decoding the genetic sequence of a virus, researchers can use computers
to compare its sequence with those of other viruses—a process known loosely
as genomics. The comparison allows drugmakers to identify genes in the new
virus that encode molecules worth targeting.
- Viruses have complex life cycles but are vulnerable to attack by pharmaceuticals
at nearly every stage.

some of the currently available antiviral drugs were developed.

After investigators decipher the sequence of code letters in a given virus, they can enlist computers to compare that sequence with those already identified in other organisms, including other viruses, and thereby learn how the sequence is segmented into genes. Strings of code letters that closely resemble known genes in other organisms are likely to constitute genes in the virus as well and to give rise to proteins that have similar structures. Having located a virus's genes, scientists can study the functions of the corresponding proteins and thus build a comprehensive picture of the molecular steps by which the virus of interest gains a foothold and thrives in the body.

That picture, in turn, can highlight the proteins—and the domains within those proteins—that would be good to disable. In general, investigators favor targets whose disruption would impair viral activity most. They also like to focus on protein domains that bear little resemblance to those in humans, to avoid harming healthy cells and causing intolerable side effects. They take aim, too, at protein domains that are basically identical in all major strains of the virus, so that the drug will be useful against the broadest possible range of viral variants.

After researchers identify a viral target, they can enlist various techniques to find drugs that are able to perturb it. Drug sleuths can, for example, take advantage of standard genetic engineering (introduced in the 1970s) to produce pure copies of a selected protein for use in drug development. They insert the corresponding gene into bacteria or other types of cells, which synthesize endless copies of the encoded protein. The resulting protein molecules can then form the basis of rapid screening tests: only substances that bind to them are pursued further.

Alternatively, investigators might analyze the three-dimensional structure of a protein domain and then design drugs that bind tightly to that region. For instance, they might construct a compound that inhibits the active site of an enzyme crucial to viral reproduction. Drugmakers can also combine old-fashioned screening methods with the newer methods based on structures.

Advanced approaches to drug discovery have generated ideas for thwarting viruses at all stages of their life cycles. Viral species vary in the fine details of their reproductive strategies. In general, though, the stages of viral replication include attachment to the cells of a host, release of viral genes into the cells' interiors, replication of all viral genes and proteins (with help from the cells' own protein-making machinery), joining of the components into hordes of viral particles, and escape of those particles to begin the cycle again in other cells.

The ideal time to ambush a virus is in the earliest stage of an infection, before it has had time to spread throughout the body and cause symptoms. Vaccines prove their worth at that point, because they prime a person's immune system to specifically destroy a chosen disease-causing agent, or pathogen, almost as soon as it enters the body. Historically vaccines have achieved this priming by exposing a person to a killed or weakened version of the infectious agent that cannot make enough copies of itself to cause disease. So-called subunit vaccines are the most common alternative to these. They contain mere fragments of a pathogen; fragments alone have no way to produce an infection but, if selected carefully, can evoke a protective immune response.

An early subunit vaccine, for hepatitis B, was made by isolating the virus from the plasma (the fluid component of blood) of people who were infected and then purifying the desired proteins. Today a subunit hepatitis B vaccine is made by genetic engineering. Scientists use the gene for a specific hepatitis B protein to manufacture pure copies of the protein. Additional vaccines developed with the help of genomics are in development for other important viral diseases, among them dengue fever, genital herpes and the often fatal hemorrhagic fever caused by the Ebola virus.

Several vaccines are being investigated for preventing or treating HIV. But HIV's genes mutate rapidly, giving rise to many viral strains; hence, a vaccine that induces a reaction against certain strains might have no effect against others. By comparing the genomes of the various HIV strains, researchers can find sequences that are present in most of them and then use those sequences to produce purified viral protein fragments. These can be tested for their ability to induce immune protection

Antiviral Drugs Today

Sampling of antiviral drugs on the market appears below. Many owe their existence, at least in part, to viral genomics. About 30 other viral drugs based on an understanding of viral genomics are in human tests.

DRUG NAMES	SPECIFIC ROLES	MAIN VIRAL DISEASES TARGETED
	DISRUPTORS OF GENOME	
abacavir, didanosine, stavudine, zalcitabine, zidovudine	Nucleoside analogue inhibitors of reverse transcriptase	HIV infection
acyclovir, ganciclovir, penciclovir	Nucleoside analogue inhibitors of the enzyme that duplicates viral DNA	Herpes infections; retinal inflammation caused by cytomegalovirus
cidofovir	Nucleotide analogue inhibitor of the enzyme that duplicates viral DNA	Retinal inflammation caused by cytomegalovirus
delavardine, efavirenz	Nonnucleoside, nonnucleotide inhibitors of reverse transcriptase	HIV infection
lamivudine	Nucleoside analogue inhibitor of reverse transcriptase	HIV, hepatitis B infections
ribavirin	Synthetic nucleoside that induces mutations in viral genes	Hepatitis C infection
	DISRUPTORS OF PROTEIN SYNTHESIS	
amprenavir, indinavir, lopinavir, nelfinavir, ritonavir, saquinavir	Inhibitors of HIV protease	HIV infection
fomivirsen	Antisense molecule that blocks translation of viral RNA	Retinal inflammation caused by cytomegalovirus
interferon alpha	Activator of intracellular immune defenses that block viral protein synthesis	Hepatitis B and C infections
	BLOCKERS OF VIRAL SPREAD FROM CELL TO CELL	
oseltamivir, zanamivir	Inhibitors of viral release	Infuenza
palivizumab	Humanized monoclonal antibody that marks virus for destruction	Respiratory syncytial infection

against strains found worldwide. Or vaccines might be tailored to the HIV variants prominent in particular regions.

Bar Entry

TREATMENTS BECOME important when a vaccine is not available or not effective. Antiviral treatments effect cures for some patients, but so far most of them tend to reduce the severity or duration of a viral infection. One group of therapies limits viral activity by interfering with entry into a favored cell type.

The term "entry" actually covers a few steps, beginning with the binding of the virus to some docking site, or receptor, on a host cell and ending with "uncoating" inside the cell; during uncoating, the protein capsule (capsid) breaks up, releasing the virus's genes. Entry for enveloped viruses requires an extra step. Before uncoating can occur, these microorganisms must fuse their envelope with the cell membrane or with the membrane of a vesicle that draws the virus into the cell's interior.

Several entry-inhibiting drugs in development attempt to block HIV from penetrating cells. Close examination of the way HIV interacts with its favorite hosts (white blood cells called helper T cells) has indicated that it docks with molecules on those cells called CD4 and CCR5. Although blocking CD4 has failed to prevent HIV from entering cells, blocking CCR5 may yet do so.

Amantidine and rimantidine, the first two (of four) influenza drugs to be introduced, interrupt other parts of the entry process. Drugmakers found the compounds by screening likely chemicals for their overall ability to interfere with viral replication, but they have since learned more specifically that the compounds probably act by inhibiting fusion and uncoating. Fusion inhibitors discovered with the aid of genomic information are also being pursued against respiratory syncytial virus (a cause of lung disease in infants born prematurely), hepatitis B and C, and HIV.

Many colds could soon be controlled by another entry blocker, pleconaril, which is reportedly close to receiving federal approval. Genomic and structural comparisons have shown that a pocket on the surface of rhinoviruses (responsible for most colds) is similar in most variants. Pleconaril binds to this pocket in a way that inhibits the uncoating of the virus. The drug also appears to be active against enteroviruses, which can cause diarrhea, meningitis, conjunctivitis and encephalitis.

Jam the Copier

A NUMBER OF ANTIVIRALS on sale and under study operate after uncoating, when the viral genome, which can take the form of DNA or RNA, is freed for copying and directing the production of viral proteins. Several of the agents that inhibit genome replication are nucleoside or nucleotide analogues, which resemble the building blocks of genes. The enzymes that copy viral DNA or RNA incorporate these mimics into the nascent strands. Then the mimics prevent the enzyme from adding any further building blocks, effectively aborting viral replication.

Acyclovir, the earliest antiviral proved to be both effective and relatively nontoxic, is a nucleoside analogue that was discovered by screening selected compounds for their ability to interfere with the replication of herpes simplex virus. It is prescribed mainly for genital herpes, but chemical relatives have value against other herpesvirus infections, such as shingles caused by varicella zoster and inflammation of the retina caused by cytomegalovirus.

The first drug approved for use against HIV, zidovudine (AZT), is a nucleoside analogue as well. Initially developed as an anticancer drug, it was shown to interfere with the activity of reverse transcriptase, an enzyme that HIV uses to copy its RNA genome into DNA. If this copying step is successful, other HIV enzymes splice the DNA into the chromosomes of an invaded cell, where the integrated DNA directs viral reproduction.

AZT can cause severe side effects, such as anemia. But studies of reverse transcriptase, informed by knowledge of the enzyme's gene sequence, have enabled drug developers to introduce less toxic nucleoside analogues. One of these, lamivudine, has also been approved for hepatitis B, which uses reverse transcriptase to convert RNA copies of its DNA

genome back into DNA. Intense analyses of HIV reverse
transcriptase have led as well to improved versions of
a class of reverse transcriptase inhibitors that do not
resemble nucleosides.

Genomics has uncovered additional targets that
could be hit to interrupt replication of the HIV
genome. Among these is RNase H, a part of reverse
transcriptase that separates freshly minted HIV DNA
from RNA. Another is the active site of integrase, an
enzyme that splices DNA into the chromosomal DNA
of the infected cell. An integrase inhibitor is now being
tested in HIV-infected volunteers.

Impede Protein Production

ALL VIRUSES MUST at some point in their life cycle
transcribe genes into mobile strands of messenger
RNA, which the host cell then "translates," or uses as
a guide for making the encoded proteins. Several drugs
in development interfere with the transcription stage
by preventing proteins known as transcription factors
from attaching to viral DNA and switching on the
production of messenger RNA.

Genomics helped to identify the targets for many
of these agents. It also made possible a novel kind of
drug: the antisense molecule. If genomic research shows
that a particular protein is needed by a virus, workers
can halt the protein's production by masking part of the
corresponding RNA template with a custom-designed
DNA fragment able to bind firmly to the selected RNA

sequence. An antisense drug, fomivirsen, is already used to treat eye infections caused by cytomegalovirus in AIDS patients. And antisense agents are in development for other viral diseases; one of them blocks production of the HIV protein Tat, which is needed for the transcription of other HIV genes.

Drugmakers have also used their knowledge of viral genomes to identify sites in viral RNA that are susceptible to cutting by ribozymes—enzymatic forms of RNA. A ribozyme is being tested in patients with hepatitis C, and ribozymes for HIV are in earlier stages of development. Some such projects employ gene therapy: specially designed genes are introduced into cells, which then produce the needed ribozymes. Other types of HIV gene therapy under study give rise to specialized antibodies that seek targets inside infected cells or to other proteins that latch onto certain viral gene sequences within those cells.

Some viruses produce a protein chain in a cell that must be spliced to yield functional proteins. HIV is among them, and an enzyme known as a protease performs this cutting. When analyses of the HIV genome pinpointed this activity, scientists began to consider the protease a drug target. With enormous help from computer-assisted structure-based research, potent protease inhibitors became available in the 1990s, and more are in development. The inhibitors that are available so far can cause disturbing side effects, such as the accumulation of fat in unusual places, but they nonetheless prolong overall health and life in many people when taken in combination with other HIV antivirals. A new generation of protease inhibitors is in the research pipeline.

Stop Traffic

EVEN IF VIRAL GENOMES and proteins are reproduced in a cell, they will be harmless unless they form new viral particles able to escape from the cell and migrate to other cells. The most recent influenza drugs, zanamivir and oseltamivir, act at this stage. A molecule called neuraminidase, which is found on the surface of both major types of influenza (A and B), has long been known to play a role in helping viral particles escape from the cells that produced them. Genomic comparisons revealed that the active site of neuraminidase is similar among various influenza strains, and structural studies enabled researchers to design compounds able to plug that site. The other flu drugs act only against type A.

Drugs can prevent the cell-to-cell spread of viruses in a different way—by augmenting a patient's immune responses. Some of these responses are nonspecific: the drugs may restrain the spread through the body of various kinds of invaders rather than homing in on a particular pathogen. Molecules called interferons take part in this type of immunity, inhibiting protein synthesis and other aspects of viral replication in infected cells. For that reason, one form of human interferon, interferon alpha, has been a mainstay of therapy for hepatitis B and C. (For hepatitis C, it is used with an older drug, ribavirin.) Other interferons are under study, too.

More specific immune responses include the production of standard antibodies, which recognize some fragment of a protein on the surface of a viral invader, bind to that protein and mark the virus for destruction by other parts of the immune system. Once researchers have the gene sequence encoding a viral surface protein, they can generate pure, or "monoclonal," antibodies to selected regions of the protein. One monoclonal is on the market for preventing respiratory syncytial virus in babies at risk for this infection; another is being tested in patients suffering from hepatitis B.

Comparisons of viral and human genomes have suggested yet another antiviral strategy. A number of viruses, it turns out, produce proteins that resemble molecules involved in the immune response. Moreover, certain of those viral mimics disrupt the immune onslaught and thus help the virus to evade destruction. Drugs able to intercept such evasion-enabling proteins may preserve full immune responses and speed the organism's recovery from numerous viral diseases. The hunt for such agents is under way.

The Resistance Demon

THE PACE OF ANTIVIRAL drug discovery is nothing short of breathtaking, but at the same time, drugmakers have to confront a hard reality: viruses are very likely to develop resistance, or insensitivity, to many drugs.

Deciphered Viruses

Some medically important viruses whose genomes have been sequenced are listed below. Frederick Sanger of the University of Cambridge and his colleagues determined the DNA sequence of the first viral genome—from a virus that infects bacteria—in 1977.

VIRUS	DISEASE	YEAR SEQUENCED
Human poliovirus	Poliomyelitis	1981
Influenza A virus	Influenza	1981
Hepatitis B virus	Hepatitis B	1984
Human rhinovirus type 14	Common cold	1984
HIV-1	AIDS	1985
Human papillomavirus type 16	Cervical cancer	1985
Dengue virus type 1	Dengue fever	1987
Hepatitis A virus	Hepatitis A	1987
Herpes simplex virus type 1	Cold sores	1988
Hepatitis C virus	Hepatitis C	1990
Cytomegalovirus	Retinal infections in HIV-infected people	1991
Variola virus	Smallpox	1992
Ebola virus	Ebola hemorrhagic fever	1993
Respiratory syncytial virus	Childhood respiratory infections	1996
Human parainfluenzavirus 3	Childhood respiratory infections	1998

Resistance is especially probable when the compounds are used for long periods, as they are in such chronic diseases as HIV and in quite a few cases of hepatitis B and C. Indeed, for every HIV drug in the present arsenal, some viral strain exists that is resistant to it and, often, to additional drugs. This resistance stems from the tendency of viruses—especially RNA viruses and most especially HIV—to mutate rapidly. When a mutation enables a viral strain to overcome some obstacle to reproduction (such as a drug), that strain will thrive in the face of the obstacle.

To keep the resistance demon at bay until effective vaccines are found, pharmaceutical companies will have to develop more drugs. When mutants resistant to a particular drug arise, reading their genetic text can indicate where the mutation lies in the viral genome and suggest how that mutation might alter the interaction between the affected viral protein and the drug. Armed with that information, researchers can begin structure-based or other studies designed to keep the drug working despite the mutation.

Pharmaceutical developers are also selecting novel drugs based on their ability to combat viral strains that are resistant to other drugs. Recently, for instance, DuPont Pharmaceuticals chose a new HIV nonnucleoside reverse transcriptase inhibitor, DPC 083, for development precisely because of its ability to overcome viral resistance to such inhibitors. The company's researchers first examined the mutations in the reverse transcriptase gene that conferred resistance. Next they turned to computer modeling to find drug designs likely to inhibit the reverse transcriptase enzyme in spite of those mutations. Then, using genetic engineering, they created viruses that produced the mutant enzymes and selected the compound best able to limit reproduction by those viruses. The drug is now being evaluated in HIV-infected patients.

It may be some time before virtually all serious viral infections are either preventable by vaccines or treatable by some effective drug therapy. But now that the sequence of the human genome is available in draft form, drug designers will identify a number of previously undiscovered proteins that stimulate the production of antiviral antibodies or that energize other parts of the immune system against viruses. I fully expect these discoveries to translate into yet more antivirals. The insights gleaned from the human genome, viral genomes and other advanced drug-discovery methods are sure to provide a flood of needed antivirals within the next 10 to 20 years.

More to Explore

Viral Strategies of Immune Evasion. Hidde L. Ploegh in *Science*, Vol. 280, No. 5361, pages 248–253; April 10, 1998.

Strategies for Antiviral Drug Discovery. Philip S. Jones in *Antiviral Chemistry and Chemotherapy*, Vol. 9, No. 4, pages 283–302; July 1998.

New Technologies for Making Vaccines. Ronald W. Ellis in *Vaccine*, Vol. 17, No. 13–14, pages 1596–1604; March 26, 1999.

Protein Design of an HIV-1 Entry Inhibitor. Michael J. Root, Michael S. Kay and Peter S. Kim in

Science, Vol. 291, No. 5505, pages 884–888;
February 2, 2001.
Antiviral Chemotherapy: General Overview. Jack M.
Bernstein, Wright State University School of
Medicine, Division of Infectious Diseases, 2000.
Available at **www.med.wright.edu/im/
AntiviralChemotherapy.html**

The Author

WILLIAM A. HASELTINE, who has a doctorate in
biophysics from Harvard University, is the chairman of
the board of directors and chief executive officer of
Human Genome Sciences; he is also editor in chief of a
new publication, the *Journal of Regenerative Medicine*,
and serves on the editorial boards of several other
scientific journals. He was a professor at the Dana-
Farber Cancer Institute, an affiliate of Harvard Medical
School, and at the Harvard School of Public Health
from 1988 to 1995. His laboratory was the first to
assemble the sequence of the AIDS virus genome. Since
1981 he has helped found more than 20 biotechnology
companies.

Web Sites

Due to the changing nature of Internet links, Rosen
Publishing has developed an online list of Web sites
related to the subject of this book. This site is updated
regularly. Please use the link below to access the list:

http://www.rosenlinks.com/saces/fidi

For Further Reading

Barry, John M. *The Great Influenza: The Epic Story of the Deadliest Plague in History*. New York, NY: Penguin, 2005.

Farmer, Paul. *Infections and Inequalities: The Modern Plagues*. Berkeley, CA: University of California Press, 2001.

Grady, Denise. *New York Times Deadly Invaders: Virus Outbreaks Around the World, from Marburn Fever to Avian Flu*. Boston, MA: Kingfisher, 2006.

Grady, Sean M. and John Tabak. *Science and Technology in Focus: Biohazards: Humanity's Battle with Infectious Disease*. New York, NY: Facts on File, 2006.

Heymann, David L., ed. *Control of Communicable Diseases Manual*. Washington, DC: American Public Health Association, 2004.

Irwin, Alexander, Joyce Millen, and Dorothy Fallows. *Global AIDS: Myths and Facts, Tools for Fighting the AIDS Pandemic*. Cambridge, MA: South End Press, 2003.

Oshinsky, David M. *Polio: An American Story*. New York, NY: Oxford University Press, 2005.

Rampton, Sheldon, and John Stauber. *Mad Cow USA: Could the Nightmare Happen Here?* Monroe, ME: Common Courage Press, 1997.

Saffer, Barbara. *Diseases and Disorders: Anthrax*. Chicago, IL: Lucent Books, 2004.

Serradell, Joaquima. *Deadly Diseases and Epidemics: SARS.* New York, NY: Chelsea House Publications, 2005.

UNAIDS. *AIDS Epidemic Update 2005.* Geneva, Switzerland: UNAIDS, 2005.

Wagner, Vigi. *At Issue: Do Infectious Diseases Pose a Serious Threat?* Chicago, IL: Greenhaven Press, 2004.

Williams, Mary E., ed. *At Issue: Vaccinations.* Chicago, IL: Greenhaven Press, 2003.

Index

viruses
  defined, 119–120
  developing resistance to
    drugs, 131–133
  mutation of, 133

W

Weill Medical College, 84, 97

Whitesides, George M., 48
Will, Robert, 64
World Health Organization,
  18, 100

Z

Zeneca, 112